True Ghost Stories

ALLAN ZULLO

D0112930

To my niece Jenna Arnold,
whose smarts and talent are matched
only by her beauty both inside and out.

CONTENTS

DO GHOSTS HAUNT BABY-SITTERS?

If you've ever baby-sat, you know how scary it can be when the kids act like spirited little demons. But some sitters have actually encountered *real* spirits and demons from the world of the supernatural.

Many experts were called in to investigate these so-called hauntings. Sometimes the experts walked away convinced that a haunting actually took place. Other times, they left believing something weird had happened that couldn't be fully explained.

This book is a collection of creepy stories about baby-sitters who took on a job that turned into the most frightening or bizarre experience of their lives. These eerie tales are inspired, in part, by real cases taken from the files of noted ghost hunters. The names and places in the stories are not real.

Could you wind up facing a ghost the next time you baby-sit? You might think so after reading the startling stories in this book!

THE
DEMON DOLL

"Caroline, have you done enough snooping around up here?" asked Sasha Arnold, wiping the sweat from her forehead. "This attic is awfully hot."

"Can't we stay here a while longer, please?" pleaded her five-year-old cousin. "There's so much fun stuff."

Sasha rolled her eyes. "Okay." She remembered the fun she'd had the first time she explored the dusty, junk-crammed attic. Ten years ago, when she was Caroline's age, Sasha had poked through the same old army trunks. She'd stared at the same heavy-framed photos of unknown people and climbed over the same leather suitcases battered from untold voyages to faraway places. Only now the attic was filled with even more cardboard boxes, many identified by labels saying "Christmas," "Halloween," and "Memorabilia."

Seeing Caroline climbing on top of a cracked, wobbly hutch, Sasha ordered, "Get down from that—" Too late. The unsteady hutch toppled backward, pitching her cousin into a pile of blankets. "Caroline!"

The little girl popped to her feet and grinned. "I'm fine! Whee, that was fun!"

"You could have been seriously hurt and I would've been very upset—not to mention in big trouble with your mom."

The blankets on which Caroline had landed slipped sideways, revealing a three-by-one-foot (0.9-by-0.3m) wooden box marked "Donny."

"What's this?" Sasha wondered. She pried it open. "Wow! Look at that!" She lifted out a boy doll that was nearly as big as Caroline. He was dressed in a white sailor outfit with a red and white striped shirt and a cocked sailor hat pinned to his hair. His head and body were made out of a thin porcelain that made his skin shine.

"I've never seen a doll that big!" marveled Caroline, reaching out to hold it. "He looks like a real boy."

Sasha fingered the doll's auburn hair. "It's the same color and texture as mine." She studied his green eyes. "They almost seem to twinkle." Painted on his pink face were freckles and the rosiest cheeks she had ever seen. "What a cute smile!"

Sasha noticed a tattoo on his right arm, partially hidden by his shirtsleeve. In small but flowery script it read "Donny." Sasha scratched her head. "I guess Donny is his name."

Handing the doll over to her cousin, Sasha reached in the wooden box and pulled out several piles of neatly folded clothes. "This is cool. He has his own wardrobe. I wonder whose doll this was."

"Oh, can I have Donny, please?" begged Caroline, squeezing the doll against her chest.

"It's not for me to say. But I guess there's no harm in taking him downstairs."

"Goody!"

"I hear the baby," said Sasha, reaching for the infant monitor that she had placed on the attic floor. "Savannah is waking up. Want me to carry the doll for you?"

"Uh-uh. He's mine. He's so sweet."

Sweet, maybe. Dangerous, absolutely.

Sasha, a willowy high-school sophomore from Iowa, was spending her spring vacation in Key West, Florida, helping her aunt Kay Arnold take care of Caroline and Savannah. Kay's husband, Dwight, was on a week-long fishing trip with his father, Andrew, in Costa Rica. Kay, an accountant, worked at home but needed Sasha to baby-sit while the live-in nanny returned to her native Sweden to attend a funeral.

The Arnolds lived in a lavender two-story wooden house. The quaint home had been built in 1896 and sat four blocks from the beach on a quiet side street lined with swaying palm trees. Sasha had been to the house before, when it was owned by her widowed grandfather. He'd sold the house to Dwight and Kay a few years ago so it would stay in the family.

While Sasha was changing Savannah's diapers, Caroline glanced out the nursery's window. "Mommy is home from her meeting. I want to surprise her. Don't tell her about Donny." With some effort, Caroline half carried, half dragged the doll downstairs to the parlor. She then set him in a wingback chair and carefully placed his hands in his lap. After adjusting his sailor cap, she stepped back and folded her arms. "There, you look like a very nice boy," she announced.

Then Caroline skipped into the kitchen to greet Kay. "Mommy, come with me. I have a new friend I want you to meet. I think you'll like him."

"A new boy in the neighborhood? I'd love to meet him."

Giggling, Caroline led Kay by the hand into the parlor. Sasha, holding the baby, followed them. "Mommy, meet Donny," said the little girl from behind the chair.

"Well, hello, Don . . . What? . . . Oh, he's not real. He's a doll—a life-sized doll!"

Caroline broke out in her trademark high-pitched laugh and eagerly asked, "Do you like him?"

"Yes. But I'm not too thrilled with his pose."

"What do you mean, Mommy?" Caroline moved from behind the chair and wrinkled her nose at the sight. The doll was leaning to the side—with his hands wrapped around his throat. "But I didn't do that, Mommy. I put his hands in his lap 'cause he's a good boy." Caroline quickly removed the doll's hands from his throat.

Kay winked at Sasha, who had her hand over her mouth to keep from laughing.

"Where did you get him?" asked Kay.

"Caroline and I were exploring the attic and we found him in a wooden box," Sasha replied. "He has six sets of clothes. Do you know whose doll he was?"

"No, I don't. I've never seen this doll before. The attic has collected so much junk over the years it's hard to know what's up there. Grandpa Andrew probably knows who the doll belongs to. When he and your uncle get back from their fishing trip, we'll ask him." Leaning down and tapping Caroline on the nose, Kay said, "In the meantime, how about taking a nap?"

"Only if Donny takes one too."

"It's a deal."

Caroline picked up Donny and carted him off to her room on the second floor. As she climbed the stairs with the doll tucked under her arm, his feet clattered on the steps.

Later that afternoon, after helping Kay feed the baby and tidying up the house, Sasha opened Caroline's door to check on her cousin. The sitter gasped in alarm.

Caroline was lying on her back, thrashing her arms and legs. The doll was sprawled out on top of her, his chest smothering the little girl's face. Sasha dashed to the bed and flung the doll off her cousin. "Caroline! Caroline!"

Caroline opened her eyes and gulped in several deep breaths. "I had a bad dream," she whimpered. "Someone covered my nose and mouth and I couldn't breathe."

Sasha sat on the edge of the bed and cradled Caroline in her arms. "You know what I think happened? You held Donny in your arms when you went to sleep. When you rolled over, he flopped over your face and made it hard for you to breathe. He's such a big doll. Maybe you should keep him in the chair when you go to sleep."

Caroline, still trying to catch her breath, nodded.

Sasha then noticed how incredibly cold it was in Caroline's room. "Aren't you freezing in here?" she asked, rubbing her bare arms.

"Yeah, I'm cold."

"It's not this bad in the rest of the house. Well, never mind. Hurry up and put your swimsuit on. Your mom's taking us to the beach."

By the time Sasha and Kay put Caroline to bed that night, the room's temperature had returned to normal. They assumed the cold was a fluke in the new central air-conditioning system that had been installed recently.

Sasha placed Donny on a chair at the foot of Caroline's bed and went to sleep in the next room. At about one o'clock, Sasha woke up to a peculiar clinking sound. It was coming from the other side of the wall that separated her room from Caroline's closet. Sasha held her breath so she could listen better, trying to identify the sound.

The clinking grew louder. *What is it?* Sasha wondered. *I've heard that sound before . . . Hey, I know. That's hangers knocking together. Caroline must be up. I'd better check.*

Sasha walked into her cousin's room and was surprised to see Caroline sleeping soundly. Then Sasha heard the hangers clink again. Goosebumps sprouted on her arms. She bravely padded over to the closet. Not knowing what she would find, the sitter flung open the door and flicked on the closet light in one quick motion.

Inside, it felt as cold as an Iowa cornfield in February. The hangers jingled as if someone had been rummaging through Caroline's clothes. But no one was in the small closet—no one except Donny the doll. He was sitting on the floor, his back propped against the wall.

"What are you doing in here?" Sasha whispered, bending down to pick him up. Before her hands touched him, he fell forward, striking his head hard against her bare feet. "Ouch!" yelped Sasha, bewildered that the doll could fall with enough force to cause such pain.

"Sasha?" mumbled Caroline.

"It's me, honey. I'm sorry if I woke you. I heard a noise and I thought it was you. Everything's fine. Um, did you stick your doll in the closet?"

"No. You put Donny on the chair, remember?"

"Yeah, you're right." *That's the problem,* Sasha thought. *I do remember leaving him on the chair. So how did he get in the closet? Maybe Kay put him there after I left the room. Or maybe Caroline did and she's too sleepy to remember.* "Go back to sleep, Caroline."

Sasha rubbed her smarting toes and bent down again to pick up the doll. The closet remained frigid even though it had no air-conditioning vent. *Where is the cold coming from?* wondered Sasha, setting the doll back on the chair.

Looking at Donny's face in the dim light from the hall, she thought his smile, which had seemed so cute earlier in the day, now looked more like a smirk. The twinkle in his eyes seemed more like a glare. *I'm beginning to have a bad feeling about this doll.*

The next morning at breakfast, Sasha learned that Kay hadn't touched the doll. Both she and Sasha assumed that Caroline had put Donny in the closet.

After Caroline woke up, she dressed Donny in a yellow shirt and brown lederhosen—Austrian leather shorts worn with suspenders. She put a dark green yodeler's hat on his head.

Later, while Kay attended a meeting at the bank, Sasha and Caroline played on the swings in the backyard. Clipped to Sasha's belt was the infant monitor, which allowed her to keep tabs on Savannah, who was sleeping in the nursery.

"Sasha, I have a joke for you. Knock, knock."

"Who's there?"

"Boo."

"Boo who?"

"Oh, don't be such a crybaby! Ha-ha!"

Sasha chuckled, not at the lame joke but at Caroline's silly laugh. When they both stopped giggling, they continued to hear laughter—a child's snickers. Sasha glanced around the backyard, then realized the sound was coming from the infant monitor.

"Savannah!" Sasha rushed into the house, knowing full well the snickers couldn't possibly be the baby's. She flew up the steps and reached the door to the nursery, but she couldn't open it.

"It's stuck!" she moaned out loud. Still hearing the laughter, Sasha lowered her shoulder and banged against the door. While frantically trying to get it open, she spotted Donny's hat on the floor a few feet away. Again and again, she threw her shoulder against the door until it reluctantly opened. Sasha bolted into the room.

To her relief, there was no intruder in the room. Sasha ran to the crib. "Not you again!" she muttered. Sitting up at the foot of the crib was Donny, flashing that once-so-cute-but-not-anymore grin. Savannah was half asleep and squirming.

"No wonder you're uncomfortable, Savannah. It's freezing in here!" Sasha opened the window to let the warm, sun-kissed air inside.

Hugging the baby, Sasha sat in a rocker, hoping the chair's motion would soothe Savannah. All the while, Sasha kept her eyes on Donny—a doll she disliked more with every passing minute.

I definitely heard a child laughing on my monitor, she told herself. *It wasn't Caroline. And Savannah is too young to make those kinds of noises. Donny can't talk . . . or can he? Geez, I'm being silly. I know he can't talk. But he's getting on my nerves. I just don't like him.*

When Caroline entered the room, Sasha asked, "Why did you put Donny in the crib with Savannah?"

"I didn't. I put him on the rocker so he could help baby-sit."

"Caroline, I found him in the crib. He didn't just climb in by himself."

Caroline shrugged and lifted Donny out of the crib. "I'll take him to my room." Acting like a mother scolding her child, Caroline waved a finger in front of the doll and said, "I told you to sit in the rocker, not the crib. You must always, always do what I say. I'm the mommy." She left the room with Donny in tow.

Minutes later, Kay returned home and went to the nursery, where Sasha was rocking the sleeping baby.

"Aunt Kay, has the nursery door ever been stuck before?" Sasha whispered.

"No, why?"

"While I was outside, I heard a child laughing on the infant monitor. I ran to the nursery, but the door was stuck. I had to hit it with my shoulder about four times before I could get in. No one was here except for the baby—and Donny. He was in the crib with her. Caroline says she didn't put him there, but how else could he have gotten in? And it was freezing in here. It's warmed up a lot in the last ten minutes."

Kay rested her hands on her hips and searched for an explanation. "Our neighbors have the same kind of monitor for their baby. Maybe our monitor picked up the sounds of one of their two older boys. As for the door, I suppose it could get stuck. It's been more humid than usual this week. Why Caroline would lie about Donny, I don't know. I'll have a talk with her. And I'll call the air-conditioning people to come out here. Oh, look. Savannah is waking up. Hi, sweet cakes."

The baby began to cry. "Ugh, you're soaked," said Sasha. "Even your top is wet." The sitter gently placed the baby on the changing table. Stripping off her top, Sasha noticed two red marks on each side of Savannah's waist. "Aunt Kay, look at this."

Kay pulled out her half glasses and examined the baby's torso. "That's odd. They look like tiny handprints. See? You can clearly make out the fingers. They're too big to be Savannah's, but they're too small to be anyone else's."

"It looks like a midget tried to grab her real hard, doesn't it?"

"Yes, I suppose so. What are you driving at, Sasha?"

"Caroline!" Sasha called out. "Would you bring Donny in here for a moment, please."

"You can't be serious," Kay told Sasha.

Caroline arrived with Donny. Sasha took the doll

and placed his hand over one of the red marks. "Aunt Kay, look. It's a perfect match."

"Maybe when he was in the crib, he fell on her and left those marks."

"I found him sitting up at the foot of the crib. Savannah was on her stomach, fussing. Aunt Kay, I have a bad feeling about Donny, a real bad feeling. I think he should be put away."

Caroline snatched the doll off the changing table. "He's my doll and you're not taking him away," she yelled.

Kay kneeled down until she was face-to-face with Caroline. "Sweetie, yesterday the doll ended up on your face and you couldn't breathe. Today, he may have hurt your baby sister. I think it's best if we put him back in the attic where you found him."

"No! He's mine! I won't let you take him!" Caroline turned to Donny. "You want to stay with me, don't you, Donny?" She put her hand behind his neck and made his head nod. "See? He wants to stay. He's my friend. I found him." She tucked the doll under her arm and hauled him back to her room.

"I don't want to upset Caroline," Kay told Sasha. "I'll let her keep Donny. But I'll make it very clear to her that the doll belongs in her room and only on the floor."

"Aunt Kay, that won't do any good. The doll is evil!"

"Your mother warned me that your imagination can run wild. Now I see what she means."

"Oh, really? Last night, the doll was supposed to

be on Caroline's chair. I found him in the closet and he attacked me—he fell right on my toes. This is after he almost smothered Caroline earlier in the day. Now, today, we see marks on the baby. And every time these things happen, it's strangely cold in the room."

"All easily explained," Kay snapped. "Enough of this silly talk."

"But, Aunt Kay—"

"Sasha, I said enough. I don't want to hear any more about this doll. Evil indeed." Kay shook her head in annoyance. She dressed Savannah and took her into the master bedroom. Meanwhile, Sasha stormed downstairs to stew in front of the television.

During "Oprah," Sasha began feeling guilty. *Maybe I was acting foolish,* she thought. *I do get carried away at times. How can a doll be evil? I shouldn't have snapped at Aunt Kay. I'd better apologize to her.*

Sasha headed up the stairs at the same time that Kay, holding Savannah, was about to come down. Looking up, Sasha said, "Aunt Kay, I'm sorry about . . . Look out for the doll!"

The warning came a split second too late. Kay tripped over Donny's prone body and lost her balance. Clutching Savannah, Kay reached out with her other hand, trying to catch herself on the bannister. But she was falling too fast. Kay twisted sideways and began sliding on her back headfirst down the stairs. But she determinedly held on to Savannah, shoving the baby onto her own chest.

Sasha frantically raced up the stairs and braced herself as Kay skidded down six steps before crashing into her. Sasha toppled over Kay and grasped Savannah's arms, preventing the baby from tumbling down the stairs.

Savannah was bawling but a quick check showed that she hadn't been hurt, because Kay's body had shielded the baby during the fall.

"She's fine, Aunt Kay. I don't know how you managed to keep Savannah from getting hurt, but you did. What about you? Are you okay?"

"I'll live." Pulling herself up, Kay slumped on the step next to Sasha. "My back and my wrist are sore, but it could have been so much worse." When she pictured how close they came to tragedy, Kay began to cry.

"Mommy?" came a frightened voice from the top of the stairs. Kay and Sasha looked up to see a tearful Caroline standing over the sprawled-out doll.

"Mommy, I'm sorry," she blurted. "I had to go to the bathroom and I couldn't take Donny with me, so I made him sit outside in the hall."

"Honey, it's okay. It was an accident."

Sobbing, Caroline ran into her room.

"Aunt Kay, I saw the doll sitting against the wall. Then he flopped forward just as you were walking by. The timing couldn't have been any worse. It was as if—" Sasha caught herself. She was afraid to say what was on her mind: *It was as if the doll tripped Aunt Kay on purpose!*

Kay limped to the top landing and flipped the doll

onto his back. She stared at his green eyes and big smile. Suddenly, they didn't seem so cute.

"Sasha, you were right about this doll," Kay said slowly but firmly. "He *is* evil. I felt a strange blast of cold air right before I tripped."

Kay's eyes glowed with anger and fear. "Get him out of here," she hissed at Sasha. "Throw him back in the attic. I don't ever want to see him again."

"What about Caroline?"

"I'll deal with her. Just get him out of my sight."

Sasha went to scoop up the doll. Maybe the terror of the last few minutes had sapped her strength, or maybe her imagination was working overtime. Whatever the reason, Donny unexplainably felt much heavier.

She lugged the doll to the attic and stuffed him in his wooden box. Then she shut the lid, shoved the box in the corner, and piled several boxes on top of it.

When she left the attic, Sasha felt a great sense of relief. Meeting up with Kay in the kitchen, she announced, "I've laid Donny to rest—for good."

If only it was that easy.

Later that evening, Sasha was baby-sitting while Kay visited a neighbor a block away. Suddenly, someone began pounding furiously on the front door and ringing the bell. "Is anyone in there?" yelled a man's voice. "Hello? Hello?"

"I'm coming, I'm coming," said Sasha. "Hold your horses."

She opened the door and recognized Mr. Perez, the next-door neighbor. "Smoke is pouring out of your attic!" he shouted. "I've called the fire department. Get everyone out now!"

The two ran up to the second floor. Mr. Perez whisked Caroline from her bed while Sasha grabbed Savannah and raced outside just as the fire trucks rolled to a stop in front of the house. Kay arrived moments later.

The firefighters soon extinguished the smoldering blaze. Fortunately, it was confined to a small area in the attic. "There was little actual fire damage," the fire chief, Captain Reynolds, told Kay. "But the things in your attic suffered major smoke damage. I hope you didn't have too many valuable things up there."

Kay shook her head blankly.

"The bedroom directly under the attic had some water damage," said the captain.

"It figures," grumbled Sasha, who was standing next to Kay, holding Caroline's hand. "That's my room."

"I had one horrifying moment," Captain Reynolds admitted. "I thought I found a dead child in the middle of the attic. My heart ended up in my throat. Then I saw it was only a big doll."

"Sir," said Sasha, "I put that doll in a wooden box in the corner. There's no way he could have ended up in the middle of the attic floor."

"That's where I found him." The captain pointed to a firefighter who was carrying Donny. "Look, there's the doll now. We thought you'd probably want

22

him. He's a lucky doll. Not a mark on him—and he was right in the middle of the fire. Isn't that amazing?"

The fireman tried to give the doll to Kay and Sasha, but neither one made any effort to take it. Finally, Caroline held out her hands and exclaimed, "Donny!"

"No!" yelled Kay. "You can't have him!"

"But, Mommy—"

"I said no!" Turning to the captain, she said, "We don't want him!"

Mrs. O'Malley, a neighbor who ran an antiques store, stepped forward from the crowd that had gathered on the sidewalk. "Mrs. Arnold," she said, "are you sure you don't want the doll? Because if you don't, I'll be glad to take it and put it in my shop."

Kay snatched the doll from the fireman and practically shoved it into Mrs. O'Malley's arms. "You want him? You got him! I don't ever want to see him again!"

Mrs. O'Malley's eyes lit up. "Thank you. Thank you very much."

"We can't figure out how the fire started," Captain Reynolds told Kay. "We saw nothing to indicate the cause. Obviously, we'll investigate further."

Two days later, Kay's husband, Dwight, and Sasha's grandfather, Andrew, returned from their fishing trip. When they learned about the bizarre events of the past week, the two men were floored.

"I knew I should've destroyed that doll," Grandpa Andrew mumbled. "He's no good. He's been bad news ever since my brother had him."

"Donny belonged to your brother?" asked Sasha.

"Yep, the doll was Hank's. He got Donny for his fifth birthday. The doll was the spitting image of him. My momma—your great-grandma Nell—knew an artist who made dolls that looked like twins of real kids. So she got him to make one for Hank. It turned out to be the worst thing she could've done for my brother.

"Hank named the doll Donny after his middle name, Donald. I hate to say this, but Hank was a rotten kid. He was always getting into trouble. A bully, a petty thief. He was eight years older than me, so he didn't pick on me too much. But everyone else was fair game. He stole lunch money from classmates, threw rocks at cats, that sort of thing. You name it, he did it.

"Whenever Hank did anything mean or bad, he always blamed it on Donny. Hank would never admit that he was at fault. It was always the doll who had done it. Over the years, that doll absorbed all of Hank's negative energy."

"What happened to Hank and the doll when he grew up?" Sasha asked.

"Hank never really grew up," Grandpa Andrew replied. "You see, he was a firebug. He was always starting fires. I can show you burns on the floors in this house where he set little blazes. If he'd had his way, he'd have burned down half of Key West. It's ironic that fire—the thing that fascinated him the most—finally killed him. He tried to torch an abandoned warehouse down at the docks. The flames spread faster than he expected, and he was trapped. He died a horrible death—and he wasn't even twenty years old.

"After Hank died, my momma wouldn't let anyone throw out Hank's things, including the doll. Donny was put in a wooden box and stored in the attic. But I should have destroyed that doll then and there, because Hank put all his bad thoughts into that demon doll.

"Sasha, once you and Caroline removed the doll from the wooden box, the negative energy was released. It infected the atmosphere in this house, causing all of you grief and aggravation. Thank goodness the doll is gone."

The next day, Sasha took Caroline for a walk. Three blocks from the house, they saw a fire truck in the street. Investigators were sifting through the rubble of a store that had burned to the ground.

Recognizing Captain Reynolds, Sasha asked, "What happened?"

"O'Malley's Antiques Store burned down during the night. Too bad. She had beautiful antiques."

"What caused it?"

"Like the fire at your aunt's house, we simply don't know. It's hard to believe we'd have such unusual fires back to back."

Sasha looked toward the charred ruins. There, in the smoking debris, she saw something that curdled her blood. A pink, rosy-cheeked, freckled face with green eyes and a wide grin.

"No, it can't be," Sasha croaked. "It's—it's Donny!"

25

LETTER FROM THE BEYOND

Mercedes Diamantis dashed to the bedroom of four-year-old Kevin Sutton the moment she heard him cry. "Kevin, what's wrong?" the baby-sitter asked.

"I had a bad dream," replied the sobbing boy.

Mercedes sat on his bed and threw her arms around him. "It must have been pretty bad for you to cry like this," she said, wiping Kevin's tears away with his sheet.

"It was about Daddy. He was on the steps of this big white building. It had a round thing on top."

Because Kevin's father, Charlie, was a political reporter, Mercedes assumed the boy was talking about the Capitol Building in Washington, where the Senate and House of Representatives meet.

"Daddy fell on the steps and got hurt real bad. People came and they tried to wake him, but he wouldn't get up."

A prickly sensation ran through Mercedes's body. She had long suspected Kevin was psychic. He once dreamed that "a policeman upset Mommy" days before she received a speeding ticket. Another time, Kevin dreamed "Daddy was in a black box and couldn't get out." A week later, Charlie was trapped in an elevator during a power failure.

In his most frightening dream, Kevin saw little green creatures attack his heart. A month later, the Suttons learned their son had a rare heart condition that would soon require major surgery.

"All my bad dreams come true," Kevin whimpered to Mercedes.

Mercedes was feeling confident and happy about life. The high-school junior was dating a jock who could actually carry on an intelligent conversation with her parents, she was acing all her classes, and she loved her new part-time job as a reporter for a suburban newspaper.

Mercedes was bummed about only one thing: The Suttons were moving to Washington, D.C. She would miss Kevin, for whom she had sat since he was an infant. She would miss his mother, Nancy, the nicest neighbor on the block. And she definitely would miss Charlie, her mentor.

Charlie was the top political reporter for the *St. Louis Post*. Two years earlier, when he found out that Mercedes was aiming for a career in journalism, he began tutoring her in the fine art of reporting.

Mercedes liked the balding, middle-aged reporter because he was quick with a quip, blunt to a fault, and never talked down to her. He insisted she call him Charlie because he hated for anyone—teen or adult—to call him "Mister."

A week after Mercedes learned that Charlie had accepted a promotion as Washington bureau chief for the *Post,* she arrived early at the Suttons' house to baby-sit.

"I have only a few minutes before Nancy and I go to this reception for a bunch of boring politicians," Charlie told Mercedes. "Let's work on your shorthand."

Over the past few weeks, he had been teaching her his own, original shorthand—a quick way to take notes. In his shorthand, he dropped vowels and used single letters, squiggles, and lines for common words.

Charlie set a small tape recorder on the table and told Mercedes, "I want you to conduct an interview with Kevin. Take down everything he says, word for word, in shorthand. Then I'll play back the tape and see how closely your shorthand matches up with what he said."

"I'm ready," said Mercedes, waving to Kevin to come into the den. After the boy sat down in the chair next to her, Mercedes said, "Kevin, I'm going to ask you some questions. How do you feel about moving to Washington?"

"I don't wanna go," he replied firmly, his dangling feet swinging back and forth.

"Why?"

"'Cause I won't have any friends."

"But you'll make new friends—and some of them will come from other parts of the world."

"I don't wanna go. I'm scared something bad is gonna happen."

"Like what?"

"I don't know. Something bad." He hopped off his chair. "I want ice cream. Will you get me some?"

"In a minute, Kevin."

Charlie turned off the tape recorder and played it back, comparing it to Mercedes's shorthand notes. "Very good, Mercedes! This is exactly what Kevin said. If you can't cut it as a reporter, you can always get a job as a secretary."

"Thanks a lot," Mercedes said in mock irritation.

"I better get going. But first, I want to give Kevin a big hug and kiss and remind him how cool it'll be living in the nation's power center."

Later that night, as Mercedes was putting Kevin to bed, she noticed he seemed unusually whiny. About two hours later, Kevin woke up screaming from the dream that his father was stricken on the steps of the Capitol Building.

When the Suttons returned home, Mercedes didn't mention Kevin's terrifying dream. She figured it would only upset them.

After paying Mercedes, Charlie said, "I probably won't be seeing you again."

Her eyes grew big as she recalled Kevin's nightmare. "Why?"

"I have to fly out Monday morning and get started at our Washington bureau. I'll be living there permanently. Nancy and Kevin will be joining me in about two months. Hopefully by then, Kevin will be strong enough to have his heart operation."

Mercedes gave him a hug. "Thanks for all your help in trying to make me a journalist."

"I expect to see you in the Washington press corps right after you get out of college."

"You better look out, Charlie. In a few years I'll be gunning for your job."

"In your dreams, young lady."

She winced at the mention of the word *dreams*. "Take care of yourself, Charlie."

Those were the last words she would ever speak to him.

The following Friday, while Mercedes was toweling Kevin off after his bath, the little boy told her matter-of-factly, "I had that dream again."

"What dream, honey?"

"The one where Daddy falls down the steps and doesn't get up."

"Sometimes we dream the same thing over and over again because it's on our minds. You probably miss your daddy a whole lot."

"Yeah, I do. I hope he's all right."

The next morning, Mercedes slept late. When she groggily trudged into the kitchen, her dark hair piled on top of her head and her rattiest robe draped over her slumped shoulders, she was surprised to see her parents looking very upset.

"Mercedes, sit down," her mother said glumly. "We have some terrible news to tell you."

Mercedes slipped into a chair and clutched her robe a little tighter. What could have happened to make her parents look so downhearted?

In a cracking voice, her mother announced, "Charlie Sutton died yesterday."

The news twisted Mercedes's stomach. She burst into tears. "Oh, no. Not Charlie! He can't be dead! Tell me this isn't happening! Oh, poor Nancy. Poor Kevin. I was going to send Charlie copies of my last two stories . . . I can't believe he's gone. How did it happen?"

Her father shoved the front page of the *Post*'s metro edition across the kitchen table. The headline read, *POST* POLITICAL EDITOR DIES IN WASHINGTON.

"Charlie suffered a massive heart attack," explained her father. "He was walking up the steps of the Capitol when he collapsed. He was dead on arrival at the hospital."

Mercedes squeezed her father's hand. "This is so unreal! Kevin's been having dreams about his father falling on the steps of a big white building with a round roof. Kevin was describing the Capitol! He said his father wouldn't get up. I kept pooh-poohing it, but Kevin's nightmare came true!"

"They think that Charlie died from the same heart condition Kevin has now," said her father.

Later that day, Mercedes and her parents visited

the Suttons' house and brought along a casserole for Nancy to share with friends and relatives who came to offer comfort.

Kevin sat on the floor in his room, playing with the Mighty Ducks action figures that Charlie had sent him from Washington. When Mercedes walked in, Kevin looked up at her and said, "My daddy isn't coming home anymore."

Fighting back her tears, she kneeled down and held him tightly. There was nothing she could say that would ease his pain—or hers.

"Mercedes, my bad dream came true. Now I'm afraid to go to sleep. What if I dream bad things about my mommy?"

Mercedes struggled to keep her composure. She sat the little boy on her lap and rocked him. "You'll have lots of nice dreams, Kevin. I promise." But as she held him, she kept thinking, *Kevin, don't have any bad dreams for a long, long time.*

Mercedes went over to the Suttons' house every day after school to be with Kevin and to free up time for Nancy to get her life back in order. About a week after the funeral, Mercedes found Nancy sitting on the floor, crying.

"The insurance company won't pay for Kevin's heart operation," Nancy wailed. "They say it's experimental. That means I have to pay over $200,000 up front before the surgery can take place. The only way I can raise that kind of money is to cash in our stocks and bonds. But I can't find them."

Pointing to the cardboard boxes piled around her, Nancy said, "These contain Charlie's personal and professional belongings. The Washington Bureau returned them to me. Mercedes, help me go through them. We need to find a key to the safe-deposit box of the new bank where he put our stocks and bonds. But I don't know the name of the bank. Without those stocks and bonds, I can't pay for Kevin's heart operation. It's a matter of life and death!"

Mercedes went through a box that held Charlie's many awards and clips of his best stories. She also found his reporter's notepads filled with his shorthand notes of interviews with the country's most powerful politicians.

Unfortunately, neither Mercedes nor Nancy found any clue to the whereabouts of the safe-deposit box key that held the only chance for Kevin's lifesaving operation.

"I don't know what I'm going to do," Nancy moaned. "I never learned what stocks and bonds we have. I don't even know who his stockbroker is."

"Mommy, what's a stockbroker?" asked Kevin, rubbing the sleep out of his eyes as he walked into the room.

"Did you have a nice nap, honey?" asked Nancy.

"Uh-huh. What are you doing?"

"We're looking through your daddy's things," answered Mercedes.

Pointing to a box labeled "Favorites," Kevin asked, "What's in there?"

"This box contains your daddy's favorite things," Mercedes replied. "See?" She pulled out several finger paintings that Kevin had made for his father. She showed him framed photos of the family, including one of Kevin shaking hands with St. Louis Cardinals all-star shortstop Ozzie Smith. The box also held photos of Charlie with presidents George Bush and Bill Clinton. "Most of your daddy's favorite things are items you made for him."

"Uh-huh," Kevin said, showing no emotion. He leaned over another box and retrieved a blank reporter's notebook. Then he picked up a pencil and walked into the kitchen.

"Nancy, how is Kevin handling things? He never talks about his father."

"I know. I'm getting a little concerned. Sometimes he seems to 'zone out,' like he's in another world. He'll take a pad of paper and start scribbling. Then he rips it up and starts all over again. He doesn't draw or write anything that makes any sense—just squiggly lines. I think he's trying to copy his father by pretending he's a reporter taking notes. The strange thing is that when I ask him what he's doing, Kevin just looks at me and says, 'Doing what?'"

Mercedes walked into the kitchen, where Kevin was hunched over the table. His tongue poking out of the corner of his mouth, the little boy was totally involved with writing in the notebook.

Mercedes poured him a glass of cranberry juice, set it on the table, and sat across from him. Leaning over until her chin nearly rested on the table, she asked, "Kevin, what are you doing?"

He ignored her. Lips pursed, eyes glazed, he remained absorbed in his writing. Scribbling for several seconds, he ripped the page out and tossed it on the floor, where at least a dozen other pages lay scattered. Then he started in on the next page, scrawling several lines before throwing that away too. It was as if Mercedes wasn't even there.

Pretending she had a telephone by her ear, she said, "Ring, ring. Hello? Is Kevin there, please? I'm trying to reach the cutest little boy on Dogwood Avenue. Hello, Kevin, are you there?"

Suddenly, Kevin put his pencil down and began breathing heavily, as if he had just run around the house. He looked across the table, smiled, and said, "Oh, hi, Mercedes."

Still holding her imaginary phone, Mercedes said, "It's nice of you to take my call, Kevin. How are you?"

Seeing that she was pretending to phone him, Kevin held a make-believe phone to his ear and replied, "Fine. How are you?"

"I brought you some cranberry juice. Why don't you drink the juice and then we'll go into the other room and play a game of Candy Land."

"Okay." Kevin hung up his imaginary phone and gulped down the juice, then hopped off his chair and headed toward the den.

"Aren't you forgetting something?" Mercedes asked him. "Before we play the game, you need to clean up the little mess you created." She pointed to the papers that lay under the kitchen table.

He looked at the pieces of paper as if he had never seen them before. "Who did that?" he asked.

"You did, goofy." Mercedes chuckled, but she was beginning to worry. She felt certain Kevin hadn't asked the question to be silly; he seemed genuinely not to know. *Maybe Nancy is right. Maybe he does need some professional help,* thought Mercedes.

Later, while Kevin and Mercedes were playing Candy Land, Nancy entered the den. "Mercedes, could you watch him for about an hour while I go down to the bank? I've got to find a way to raise that money."

"Sure, no problem, Nancy."

Mercedes stepped outside the room with Nancy and whispered, "I see what you mean about Kevin. He didn't even realize he had been scribbling in his father's notebook. For that matter, he didn't even know I was sitting across the table from him for several minutes."

"I think I'll call a child psychologist tomorrow," said Nancy. "This can't go on much longer."

After Nancy left, Mercedes returned to the den. Kevin was sitting on the floor, writing in his father's notebook again.

"Kevin," said Mercedes. "Kevin?" She received no reply. Once again, the little boy seemed to be in a trance as he scribbled furiously. Every few seconds, he would rip up a page and begin on a fresh one.

Mercedes picked up one of the pages and glanced at it. She was about to throw it away when she noticed the top line looked suspiciously like Charlie's unique shorthand. She studied it closely. The first two words looked like they could mean "Sugar Pie." Maybe Kevin was trying to copy a line from one of his dad's notebooks.

Then Mercedes examined the next line. It too had the shortened words and squiggles that made up Charlie's shorthand. Her heart beating faster, Mercedes sat down and studied the piece of paper. Methodically, she translated the shorthand symbols into letters:

Sgr Pi, stox n sf dpst bx @ Ct Nat Bk Conn
Av. Ky in Oz Sm pix. Lv, C.

"I think I've got it!" she shouted out loud. "Yes! I know what this says!"

She grabbed a clean sheet of paper and printed out the first part of the message: "Sugar Pie, the stocks are in a safe-deposit box at City National Bank on Connecticut Avenue." Then she figured out most of the second part: "Key in Oz Sm picture. Love, Charlie." *Key in Oz Sm? What's that mean? Oz Sm? Oz Sm? Of course, the Ozzie Smith photo!*

Mercedes darted into the living room and rifled through the box containing the framed picture. She opened the backing and out fell a thin key with a number stamped on it—a safe-deposit box key!

"This is absolutely incredible!" Mercedes cried. But her happiness quickly turned to confusion. *Kevin doesn't know shorthand,* she thought. *He can barely print his name. How could he have written this? Maybe*

Charlie wrote it in his notebook before he died. Of course, that's what happened.

She ran back into the den, where Kevin had finished writing and was watching television. "Are you finished writing?" she asked him.

The little boy looked at her as if he didn't know what she was talking about, then shrugged and looked back at the TV. Meanwhile, Mercedes gathered up the other pieces of paper he had scribbled on and examined them. They were nearly identical, all carrying the same message in Charlie's shorthand. She went into the kitchen and dug through the trash can, pulling out the other pages that Kevin had written on. They too had the identical shorthand message.

Kevin must have copied Charlie's note over and over. But I saw him write it several times without looking at any of the other pages. How did he do that?

She went into the den with the notebook and a pencil and asked Kevin, "Would you write me the same message that you've been jotting down in your daddy's notebook?"

He took the notebook and pencil and began writing. When he finished, he handed it back to her. She examined it carefully but it was nothing but childish scrawls. It certainly wasn't shorthand.

"No, Kevin. I want you to write like this," she said, pointing to one of the pages that contained the shorthand he had written earlier.

"I don't know how to write, Mercedes. You know that."

"Just try."

Moments later, he handed her a page with jumbled printed block letters that said KEVIN SUTTON.

Just then, Nancy returned home. Mercedes excitedly broke the news of how she had discovered the key and showed Nancy the pages of shorthand that Kevin had written.

Nancy buried her head in her hands and wept. When she collected herself, she declared, "The message couldn't have come from Kevin."

"But I saw him write it."

"It wasn't him, Mercedes."

"How can you say that?"

"Because of the way the message begins. 'Sugar Pie' was Charlie's pet name for me. He never called me that in front of anyone—even Kevin."

"So how do you explain what Kevin wrote?"

Nancy smiled through her tears. "Charlie's spirit wrote that message. Don't you see, Mercedes? He sent it to me through Kevin's hand! Charlie needed to get the message about the safe-deposit key to me—and going through our psychic son was the best way. Charlie's spirit guided Kevin's hand.

"Charlie wanted to make sure that we'd find the money for Kevin's heart operation. He always thought of us. And he still is—even from the beyond."

Three months later, Kevin underwent the delicate and expensive heart operation. It was a complete success.

THE SECRET GRAVE

July 12

Dear Diary,

I'm going to Woodstock, Vermont, for twelve days! It won't cost me anything, plus I get paid $150!! The Pulaskis asked me to come with them on their summer vacation. I leave tomorrow. We're flying from Jacksonville to Boston and then taking a rental car to a farmhouse in the country! An excellent adventure for a thirteen-year-old like me. Jax in the summertime is super yucky. Vermont will be so COOL—in more ways than one.

The downside to this trip: I have to baby-sit Anna. She's not my favorite kid. But as eight-year-olds go, I guess she's not too bad, although she *is* a whiner and a scaredy-cat.

Remember, Diary, last year when she had me convinced there was a burglar in the house and I called 911? I almost DIED from embarrassment when the cops came and saw that every window and door had been locked and there was no way a burglar could get in. The Pulaskis didn't ask me to sit for Anna for months after that!

In fact, I was surprised they asked me to go to Vermont with them. But their regular sitter couldn't go at the last minute. The Pulaskis were so desperate they probably called a hundred sitters before they thought, *Michelle Roberts is our last hope.* They sure seemed happy when I said yes.

As you know, Diary, this summer has been BORING. We hang out at the swim center, we hang out at the mall, we hang out at each other's house. It's the same-old, same-old. So when the Pulaskis asked me to go with them, I was, like, already there in my mind. Mom said it was okay if I went. I'm packed and so PSYCHED. Tonight Jax . . . tomorrow Woodstock!

July 13
Dear Diary,

We made it to Woodstock! It's been a long day. The flight was smooth, but the drive from Boston wasn't. Mr. P got lost driving out of the airport and Mrs. P kept yelling at him. I hope they don't bicker like that the whole time we're in Vermont or it'll be a long twelve days.

Anna was cranky. She whined about being hungry and thirsty and then complained of a stomachache and a headache. I tried to keep her busy playing games.

If my writing looks bad it's because I'm using a flashlight in bed. I share a bedroom with Anna, and she's asleep in the bed next to me.

Let me tell you about this rented cabin: It's so COOL!! It's over two hundred years old. It's made out of split logs and has wood floors and low ceilings. Antiques are everywhere: handmade quilts, hand-carved chairs and tables, old pictures of people from way back when, and even a wood-burning, pot-bellied stove in the kitchen. Thank goodness the cabin has electricity and indoor plumbing. There are two bedrooms, a teeny-tiny bathroom, a kitchen, and a big room that doubles as a dining room and living room. I almost had a heart attack when I thought the place didn't have a TV. But it does—cable with HBO!

Believe it or not, there's an outhouse in the back. How could anyone use that? Especially in the winter! There are also a couple of old sheds and run-down farm buildings on the property. Tomorrow we'll go exploring.

Oh, and here's the best part: The lady who rented out this place whispered to me that it's HAUNTED!!! I think she was joking, but I'm not sure. What would I do if I saw a ghost? Scream!!

July 14
Dear Diary,

We all went on a short hike around this old farm. Very nice. We saw a deer! It was a doe. She was so pretty. We startled her and she bounded into the woods like she had springs on her feet.

I never knew deer could jump that far.

We found a family cemetery about a ten-minute walk past the farm buildings. The gravestones were really old and some were hard to read. Wadsworth seems to be a popular name.

Anna is a pain. She kept whining today. Probably because she didn't get a whole lot of sleep last night. That meant I didn't either. It's partly because the beds are hard as tombstones. And it's partly because Anna gets spooked by everything.

She kept whimpering all night that someone was in the room. Yeah, Anna. I was in the room, trying to get some sleep!! She claimed someone had pulled the covers off her bed. Then she said someone had grabbed her toes. Then she said someone had shoved her bed. I felt like shoving Anna myself—right out of the room.

July 15
Dear Diary,

We all went into town today to do some shopping because it's been raining. At a bookstore, the Pulaskis talked to an old man who had written a book about ghosts in the area.

I tried to get Anna away from him because I was sure she would freak if she thought there were ghosts floating around here. But she put up a stink and wanted to hear what the man had to say. He wanted to tell us something about our house, but Mrs. P gave him the brush-off and we left. The Pulaskis don't believe in ghosts.

Anna says our place is haunted. When we got home, she kept asking us if ghosts would harm her and we said no. We had her convinced when suddenly the lights went out. Boy, did that freak her! I got spooked a little too because it happened right after Mr. P said, "There are no such things as ghosts." We played hearts by candlelight.

The worst part about not having electricity here is that you can't use any water. The water comes from the well, which needs an electric pump to push the water through the faucets. So we don't have any water to brush our teeth or even flush the toilet. The Pulaskis use the outhouse. Not me. I'm holding it until the power comes back on. It better be on by morning!!

FLASH: The weirdest thing just happened. I heard a sound like someone tapping on the walls. It grew louder and louder. I thought it might be water in the pipes and that maybe the power had come back on, but it hadn't. The tapping was coming from the wall near Anna's bed and it woke her up. I used the flashlight, but we couldn't find any reason for the tapping. There's just a hallway on the other side of the wall, and there was nothing out there. Then the tapping stopped.

I told Anna that the noise was just water draining from the pipes, and she believed me. But it really sounded like someone was tapping on the wall with their knuckles. Anna is asleep now. I better get to sleep too.

July 16

Dear Diary,

We went horseback riding today in the Green Mountains. It was awesome! My horse, Midnight, wanted to gallop, but all we could do was trot a little on the trail. We found some cool views, and we had a picnic in a meadow. It was right out of a picture book. A very pretty day.

The power finally came back before we got home from horseback riding. Thank goodness!! This morning I had to go so bad that I used the outhouse. Pee-uuu!! I held my breath the whole time—which wasn't very long. While I was in there, I heard that same tapping sound from last night. It stopped the moment I opened the door. I ran around the outhouse, but I didn't see anyone. Must be some kind of animal.

Oh, I almost forgot. The man from the bookstore stopped by this afternoon. He was talking with Mr. P outside. Mr. P asked me to take Anna inside, which I did. I turned on the TV, and while she was watching it, I leaned by the open window and heard them talking about a ghost! The old man said that other renters of this house have seen the ghost of a young woman roaming around the porch! I don't know if he was trying to scare the Pulaskis or wanted them to buy his book. The Pulaskis didn't say a word about the ghost at the dinner table tonight. Maybe this cabin is haunted!

*   *   *

July 17
Dear Diary,

It's 7:30 in the morning. But if I don't put this down right now, I'm going to bust! We saw a GHOST!!

Last night I was sound asleep when Anna woke me up. It was about 1:30 A.M. We could hear the tapping noise again, only this time it was coming from the ceiling. Anna told me that someone had taken off her covers, grabbed her toes, and then shoved her bed—just like the first night here.

I thought it was nonsense, but we both heard the tapping. Then Anna complained of a bad chill. I felt it too. It was a creepy kind of chill, not like a cold breeze or anything. (The bedroom window was closed.) The chill stayed around Anna's bed. I had a feeling that someone else was in the room, but I didn't say anything to Anna because I didn't want to scare her.

Then she gasped and pointed over my shoulder. We both saw her. A young woman in her early twenties was standing between the door and the bed! She didn't move a muscle. She just stared at us with these very large, very sad eyes.

I was petrified!! Moonlight from the window shone on her—that's why we could see her. She was dressed in very old-fashioned clothes—a plain ankle-length dress and an apron. Nothing like we wear today. Her hair was very long and reached to her waist.

She kept staring at us. Finally, I asked, "What do you want?" The woman didn't say a word. I got freaked and Anna did too. She dived under the covers and screamed her lungs out, so I turned on the light. But as soon as the light went on, the woman vanished! It was SO SPOOKY!!

The Pulaskis came into the room and we told them what happened. They weren't too thrilled to hear our story because, as you know, they don't believe in ghosts. We had no proof that we saw a ghost, except we know that we did. Who she was and why she was here, I don't know. I think the Pulaskis blamed me for Anna being so scared. But I was scared too. I still am!

We left the hall light on and we kept the bedroom door wide open. Anna and I didn't get much sleep.

July 17—Later
Dear Diary,

We had fun today hiking to a waterfall. Then we drove around and saw two covered bridges. I was impressed. Anna wasn't.

Time to turn in. I hope we don't see *her* again tonight. Anna is kind of afraid. The Pulaskis made it clear that they don't want to hear us babbling about ghosts.

July 18
Dear Diary,

It's about 2:00 A.M. I'm sitting out here under the hall light to write this because I'm too nervous to sleep, and I want to write down everything so I won't forget the details in the morning.

I SAW THE GHOST AGAIN!!

Anna did too, but she actually slept through most of the ghost's visit.

Around midnight, I woke up because I felt I was being watched. The light was on in the hall and the door was open. At first I didn't see anyone. Then I felt very cold. It was like you're leaning over the side of a cliff and looking straight down thousands of feet and you get the chills. Only this was a hundred times more intense.

Suddenly, out of nowhere, the ghost appeared. She was dressed in the same clothes and she had the same sad look on her face. I'll never forget her eyes. They looked like they were pleading for help. She was obviously very upset.

I don't know why, but I didn't seem nearly as scared as I was last night. Maybe it's because I don't think she's here to hurt me or Anna. I think she came to us for help. I told her, "Talk to me. Tell me who you are and what you want." But she didn't reply. So I tried to be friendlier and said, "Is something bothering you? I'll help you if you'll just let me know what I can do for you."

I still couldn't get the ghost to talk. I was getting a little frustrated. Meanwhile, Anna began waking up. I hopped over to her bed, which was a good thing, because when she woke up and saw the ghost, she started to scream. But I put my hand over her mouth so she wouldn't wake up her parents. Besides, I didn't want her scaring away the ghost. When Anna calmed down, I took my hand away from her mouth. I promised her the ghost wouldn't harm us (even though I don't know for sure if that's true).

Anna asked the ghost, "Who are you?" Suddenly, an old book fell off the shelf near our beds. By the time the book hit the floor, the ghost had disappeared.

It was a real old book of poetry called The Meadow of Sorrow. The poems were all sad ones about death and lost loves. I don't know if they have anything to do with the ghost. A name was written inside the front cover—Helen Wadsworth. There were a bunch of Wadsworths buried out in the cemetery. Could that be the name of the ghost?

I convinced Anna not to tell her parents about what happened. I think it's best if we keep it to ourselves.

It's 9:30 P.M. on the same day. Anna is reading in bed. I'm in bed too.

Today we went on another hike, but Anna whined a lot because the trail went up a mountain. It was hard even for me, and I'm in pretty good shape.

In the afternoon, Anna and I stayed at the cabin while Mr. and Mrs. Pulaski went on a long bike ride. I thought it would be a perfect time to have the ghost pay us a visit. Things don't seem so scary in the daytime. We went into our bedroom and asked out loud for the ghost to appear. She didn't show—not even after I asked for Helen Wadsworth.

Then Anna and I went to the cemetery. We found Helen Wadsworth's grave! Her tombstone is in pretty bad shape, but we could still read that she was born in 1852 and died in 1875. The ghost we saw in our bedroom looked like she could be twenty-three years old. Very interesting, wouldn't you say, Diary?

Then we played hide and seek. I let Anna hide first. I couldn't find her anywhere and I was starting to get a little panicky. I finally found her hiding in the woodshed. She was crying. I mean, major waterfall.

I asked her what was wrong and she said she didn't know. She just felt very, very sad. Then I realized that I was feeling pretty down too—kind of like how I felt at Uncle Bud's funeral. Real depressed. But there was no reason for us to feel this way.

We were leaving the woodshed when we heard that same strange tapping sound. I ran around the shed in one direction and Anna ran the opposite way. We met in the back, but we didn't find anyone. Once we got away from the woodshed, we didn't feel so depressed. Weird, huh?

This place gets creepier and creepier!! Will the ghost show up tonight? Stay tuned . . .

July 19
Dear Diary,
WOW! It's bombshell time!
We were in town and the Pulaskis were visiting antiques shops, so they gave Anna and me money for ice cream and told us to meet them in an hour at the

park. Who should we see at the ice cream shop but the old man from the bookstore. His name is Burgess Kinnard.

He remembered us and I told him I saw him out at the cabin. I asked him if he thought the place was haunted, and he said, "Most definitely." He said the Pulaskis didn't believe him when he told them. I asked him to tell us what he knew about this place.

Mr. Kinnard said that over the years, people who have stayed in the house have seen the ghost of a young woman who seems very sad. (Does that sound familiar??) She just comes and goes and no one can get her to talk.

Anna told him that we had seen the ghost too. He got real excited to hear that. I told him about the book that had fallen during the ghost's visit. Mr. Kinnard just about fell off his stool when I mentioned Helen Wadsworth's name was written on the inside cover.

It seems the house was owned for generations by the Wadsworth family. In the 1800s, Helen spent time in a mental institution. Some people said she was crazy, but others thought she was simply odd. She made a living making jewelry and gold bracelets. She got married and soon got pregnant. But then her husband died in a hunting accident. Her relatives worried that she wouldn't be able to take care of the baby alone, so they made plans to have someone else raise the child once it was born.

In 1875, Helen gave birth to a boy, John, but he

wasn't very healthy. Helen's relatives tried to convince her to give up the baby for adoption, but she refused. She grabbed a gun and ordered everyone off her property. About a week later, they came back. Helen was very sick with a high fever. They couldn't find the baby anywhere. They kept asking Helen about Baby John, but she was out of it from the fever. She slipped into a coma and died. They buried her in the family plot. To this day, no one knows what happened to the baby.

July 20
Dear Diary,

This was the most unbelievable day of my life!! Looking back on everything that happened today, I feel like I've been living in a movie instead of real life. I'm still so full of mixed-up feelings that I probably won't sleep for a week.

This morning, the Pulaskis went on one of their marathon bike rides in the countryside, so Anna and I stayed here at the house. About ten o'clock this morning, we were playing checkers out on the back porch when Anna screamed and pointed toward the woodshed. There was HELEN'S GHOST!!

She was standing in front of the woodshed, wringing her apron and crying. She looked down toward her feet and shook her head. Then she bent down and smoothed the dirt with her hands. We didn't say a word. We just watched. She stood up, blew the ground a kiss and then—poof!—she was gone.

We ran over to the woodshed, but we didn't want to get too close. I wondered why the ghost was smoothing the dirt and blowing it a kiss. I told Anna that I thought something might be buried there, and she said, "The baby?"

All of a sudden, I burst out crying. I had that awful sad feeling again—just like the other day in the woodshed. I ran away from the shed and immediately felt better.

I believed the answer to why the woodshed was so depressing was buried in the spot where Helen's ghost had been. I found a shovel in the barn and walked into the woodshed. I began to feel sad again, but I tried not to let it get to me. I had Anna stay outside and read me funny jokes and riddles from one of the books she had brought while I started digging. It took less than five minutes before I hit something. Tears began streaming down my face. I fell to my knees and began pushing dirt aside. Then I screamed. It was a tiny human skull!

I should have run, but I couldn't. Even though I was very upset and crying, I kept on digging with my hands, and I found small bones and a little gold bracelet. It was still very shiny. I held it up to the sunlight and saw it was engraved. It said JOHN W., 1875. I was pretty sure we had just discovered the grave of Helen's baby—John Wadsworth!

Anna and I sat in front of the woodshed and cried for the poor little thing.

We didn't know what to do, so I called Mr.

Kinnard at the bookstore. He came right out with the police. They examined the bones and said it was probably the skeleton of a baby who had died a long time ago. When the police chief asked me what made me dig in front of the woodshed, I didn't know what to say. So I told him about Helen's ghost. He walked away shaking his head—even after Mr. Kinnard said he believed me and Anna.

Before the cops took the skeleton away, the Pulaskis came back. They just about had a heart attack when the cops explained what had happened.

Mrs. P was so upset she wanted to leave for home right then, but Mr. P talked her into staying. They were afraid Anna would turn into a head case from seeing the ghost and baby. But Anna seems cool about it. Not that she or I are really all that calm.

It's a little before midnight now, and Anna is still awake. We're waiting for Helen's ghost to show up. I hope she does.

July 21
Dear Diary,

We took a day trip to Manchester today. Everyone was pretty quiet in the car and no one said much about the ghost. What's that expression? Out of sight, out of mind.

Anna had asked me if I saw the ghost last night, and I said I hadn't. Mrs. P said that we shouldn't talk about it anymore.

This afternoon a newspaper reporter called, but

Mr. P wouldn't let her talk to us. He answered a few questions and then hung up.

I wonder what has happened to Helen's ghost.

July 22
Dear Diary,

A bummer of a day. Lots of rain and wind.

The police chief, Mr. Kinnard, and some officials came out to the house today and asked us more questions. Mr. Kinnard thinks the baby died of natural causes and that Helen went out of her mind in grief and buried the baby in the woodshed.

They plan to rebury Baby John in the family plot tomorrow. The local funeral home has donated a coffin, and Mr. Kinnard's son, who's a sculptor, is making a little gravestone. The funeral is a good idea. I think that's what Helen's ghost wanted us to do all along.

Mrs. P doesn't want us at the funeral, but Anna put up such a fuss that Mr. P said it was okay.

Helen, where are you?

July 23
Dear Diary,

Dozens of people showed up for Baby John's funeral. I guess they read about it in the newspaper. It was a short, sweet ceremony. A minister said a few words, and then they lowered the coffin into the ground right next to where Helen was buried. Some of the people placed flowers on Baby John's grave and on Helen's too.

Anna and I got teary-eyed. It was sad in a way. But it was also nice too, because now Baby John is closer to his mother. I'm pretty sure that's what Helen wanted. I was hoping that she would show up at the funeral. Anna and I kept looking for her, but we didn't see her.

I'd like to see her again. This is our last night here—we leave for home tomorrow morning. It's 11:30 P.M.

Helen, please show up!

July 24
Dear Diary,

I saw her!! I saw her!!

It's about 1:00 A.M. now. Helen appeared just a few minutes ago! I had fallen asleep after writing to you, Diary, when I woke up just like that. Anna woke up at the same time. We both sat up for no reason, and then Helen appeared by the door.

She looked so different. She was still wearing the same clothes, but it was like she was a whole new person. Her eyes sparkled and she had a smile on her lips. She seemed relieved and not at all troubled.

Anna told her, "I'm sorry about your baby."

I told Helen, "I hope we did the right thing."

She held out her hands and gave us a big smile. Then she faded away.

Good-bye, Helen. May you rest in peace.

THE UNINVITED

THUMP . . . BANG . . . BANG . . . THUMP . . . THUMP . . . BANG.

"What are those darn kids up to now?" muttered Emily Templeton. The fourteen-year-old baby-sitter hopped off the couch and stormed upstairs to the room of brothers Matthew and Michael Curry. "They promised me they would be good tonight."

THUMP . . . BANG . . . BANG . . . THUMP . . . THUMP . . . BANG.

Emily whipped open their door, took one step into the room—and froze in shock. "I—I d-don't believe what I'm seeing!" she gasped.

Emily had been the boys' only sitter since the Curry family moved into the trim, red and white brick colonial on Loblolly Lane.

Everyone in the neighborhood was glad to see the

Currys move in. The home's previous owners, Mr. and Mrs. Enfield, were crotchety, nasty people who would throw a fit if anyone stepped foot on their property. No matter how nice passersby were to them, the unsmiling Enfields ignored them. After the Enfields moved to Arizona, neighbors held a block party to welcome the Currys—and to celebrate the departure of the Enfields.

Mike, eight, and Matt, seven, could almost pass for twins. They sported the same buzz haircuts, pug noses, mischievous smiles, and wide eyes. They were always in constant motion, unleashing enough energy to power an entire city block.

As an experienced baby-sitter, Emily knew the Curry boys were at their peak troublemaking years. The second time she sat for them, she thought she could win them over by joining in their favorite games. The trio played dodgeball in the driveway until Emily got whacked in the face with the ball, knocking her glasses off and bruising her nose.

They switched to a fast-paced squirt-gun fight in the backyard. When Emily was about to nail Mike, Matt ran behind her, grabbed a Super-Soaker hidden in the bushes, and drenched her. The ambush turned her short curly brown hair into a limp mop. It also signaled the end of the game. After she toweled off and had her mother bring over a dry set of clothes, Emily suggested they play a less physical game like Clue.

She went into the kitchen to make popcorn first.

In the family room, Colonel Mustard and Professor Plum slipped off the game board. Mike accused Matt of knocking them off. Matt claimed he hadn't touched the board. The two began arguing and hurling tokens at each other until Emily came in and broke up the fight.

"Pick up the pieces and put the game away," she ordered. "I'm very disappointed in you two."

"Hey, I smell something burning," said Mike.

"Oh, my gosh! The popcorn!" Emily rushed into the kitchen and found the popcorn popper on fire. The boys whooped and ran around with their mouths open, trying to catch flying popcorn with their tongues. Meanwhile, Emily unplugged the appliance and poured salt on the small flame.

"Wait until our parents see this," Mike sniggered.

"But I had just turned it on," said Emily. "It didn't even have time to heat up." *This is turning into one of those baby-sitting jobs that makes me wonder if I ever want to raise a family,* Emily told herself. *Strike that thought. Keep cool. Only a couple more hours before the Currys come home.*

After watching a movie on TV—Emily refused to let them see *Friday the 13th*—the boys faced bedtime. To her relief, they went upstairs without a peep and brushed their teeth. Then they returned to give her a hug. "You're a fun sitter," praised Mike. "Will you come back again?"

I'm not sure I ever want to sit for them, Emily thought. *But they look so sweet in their pajamas, and*

it was nice of them to come down and say good night.
"Sure I will, if your parents ask me."

The boys went back upstairs and hopped into bed. Meanwhile, as Emily nestled on the couch, she felt something crawling between the cushion and her back. She turned around and shrieked. A green snake was slithering on the cushion. "Those little devils!"

Once the shock wore off, Emily realized the creature was a harmless garter snake. She wasn't very fond of snakes, so she used a long barbecue fork to pick it up and then marched to the boys' room. They were both in their beds, pretending to be asleep.

Emily tossed the snake on Mike's bed. "Very funny, guys. You got me good with the snake."

"Huh?" said Mike, blinking his eyes. "What are you doing with Slinky?"

"As if you didn't know," she snapped.

"We don't," claimed Matt.

"While one of you hugged me downstairs, the other slipped the snake onto the couch," said Emily. "Well, it worked. You scared the air right out of my lungs."

"We didn't do it, honest," Mike claimed. "Slinky was in his tank with Herbie and Viper."

"You mean, there are more snakes?"

"Yeah, look for yourself." He got out of bed, turned on the light, and pointed to a glass tank in the corner. "Oh-oh. Matt, do you know where Herbie and Viper are?"

"They were in there a few minutes ago."

"Are they garter snakes too?" Emily asked.

"No, they're black and much larger," Mike replied. "Herbie and Viper are as long as a yardstick. And thick too. We'd better look for them."

Emily didn't like what she was hearing. If the boys were pulling a prank and there were no other snakes, they were doing a great acting job. There wasn't a hint of a smile on either boy.

"One of two things has happened here," she said. "Either you deliberately let out your snakes or you're making up a story. Which is it?"

"Neither," said Matt. "They escaped. We didn't let them out."

Hurry up and come home, Mr. and Mrs. Curry, Emily thought. *I don't want to sit for these pint-sized jerks anymore.*

"We need to find our snakes," Mike declared.

"Okay, I'll give you guys ten minutes to round them up. Then it's back to bed."

Thirty minutes later, they still hadn't found the reptiles—if, in fact, they even existed. Emily finally sent the boys to bed after getting them to promise they would not cause any more trouble. Then she sat on a chair, keeping her feet off the floor just in case those allegedly missing snakes slithered into the room.

About an hour later, Emily heard THUMP . . . BANG . . . BANG . . . THUMP . . . THUMP . . . BANG coming from upstairs. "Emily, get up here quick!" yelled Mike.

"I wonder what those darn kids are up to now?" Emily muttered. The annoyed sitter stormed up the stairs, expecting another practical joke. She whipped open the door—and couldn't believe her eyes.

"Look!" shouted Matt. He pointed to the desk chair, which was jerking slowly across the floor.

"Oh, my gosh!" Emily cried out. "It's moving by itself!"

The chair hit the wall and flipped over, its legs pointing toward the ceiling. "It doesn't seem possible!" she exclaimed. Prepared to flee at the slightest movement of the chair, the tense sitter walked up to it. She relaxed after seeing a rope dangling from the back. "What's this?"

"That's a rope," said Mike. "Earlier today we tied it from the chair to the bed and used it as a net to play volleyball on our knees with a Nerf ball."

Emily shook her head and smirked. "Now I get it. Somehow you rigged this chair to make it look like it was moving by itself. And I fell for the gag."

"But we didn't touch the rope," Matt declared.

"So what you're saying is that the chair actually moved across the floor on its own." The boys nodded. "Fine. I'll solve this." She picked up the chair and carried it out to the hallway. "There, you won't have to worry about that chair anymore. Let's knock off the jokes, okay?"

Stomping down the stairs, Emily thought, *I can't wait until I'm older and don't have to baby-sit anymore.*

When she reached the bottom, she heard thumping and bumping in the upstairs hall. She bounded back up and discovered the chair was now down at the other end of the hall, far from the boys' room. *The rope is only a few feet long,* she thought. *How could the boys have moved it while they stayed in their room?*

Spotting the boys peeking out from behind the door, Emily applauded. "Boys, this trick is the best ever. How'd you do it?"

"We didn't, Emily," Mike maintained. "No lie."

Later, when the Currys returned home, Emily told them about the popcorn maker fire. Mr. Curry figured it had been caused by a short in the wiring.

"Do the boys have more than one snake?" asked Emily.

"Yes, they have three," Mrs. Curry replied. "Why?"

"The garter snake got out of its cage, but I found it. The bigger black snakes are still missing."

Mrs. Curry laughed. "The boys don't have any big black snakes. All three are little garter snakes that always get out—and we can't figure out how."

"One other thing," said Emily. "The boys' desk chair is out in the hallway. They said it moved on its own. Naturally, I figured they were playing a prank on me. So I set the chair in the hall."

The Currys gawked at each other. Looking at their faces, Emily saw they were terrified.

Against her better judgment, Emily agreed to baby-sit for the boys a week later. The Currys paid very well, and she was desperate to earn enough money to buy a leather jacket.

"I've had a long talk with the boys," Mrs. Curry told Emily. "They assured me they won't cause you any trouble. But I must warn you, they aren't themselves. It must be the move. Ever since we arrived here, the kids have been hearing strange noises, and they've been breaking each other's toys and squabbling all the time. I think they're having a tough time adjusting. Please keep that in mind."

"Thanks for letting me know," said Emily. "I'll be more understanding."

After the Currys left, Emily sat on the family-room floor with the boys, who were playing with their plastic Lego building bricks.

"How do you like living here?" she asked.

"It's all right," Mike replied. "I'm not crazy about the house."

"Me neither," Matt piped in.

"Why not?" Emily asked.

"This house is spooked," Mike insisted. "Furniture moves on its own. You saw our chair move. That was no joke."

"Our things disappear and then they show up in weird places," Matt told her. "Our remote-control car vanished and Dad found it in his underwear drawer. Both our G.I. Joes were in the washing machine—and we didn't put them there. And all the aces are missing from our deck of cards."

"We hear banging and scraping noises at night,"

added Mike. "Mom and Dad hear them too. The other day, our chair moved again. When we woke up, it was in the guest room."

"What happened to your snakes?" asked Emily, still doubting the boys' outlandish story.

"We were kidding you about how big they were," Matt admitted. "All three are garter snakes. They're always escaping. We put a dictionary on top of the plastic cover on the cage and they still got out. We never did find the other two garter snakes."

Seeing that the boys were downhearted, Emily said cheerily, "Let's build a house out of these Legos. We'll make it the kind of place you would love to live in."

The boys soon created a three-story house complete with an indoor pool, media room, and rooftop basketball court. "Great job, boys!" beamed Emily. She opened the front door of the Lego house and said, "Now pretend you're stepping into your new home."

Before they could kick their imaginations in gear, the Lego house blew apart, spewing Lego bricks in all directions. Legos bounced off the boys as they dived for cover. Emily was struck in the forehead and chin before she dropped to the floor.

The boys stared in open-mouthed amazement at the ruins of their Lego house. Their fearful, puzzled eyes then glanced at Emily, who could barely move from the shock.

"Is everyone okay?" After the boys nodded—not

very convincingly—she wondered out loud, "What just happened?"

"Our house exploded!" Matt bawled.

"Did one of you plant a cherry bomb inside?" But Emily knew they hadn't because there weren't any loud bangs or burn marks. "No, I guess not."

Matt tried to hold back his tears, but he was fighting a losing battle. "Why did our Lego house blow up?"

"I don't like it here," Mike sniveled. "I want to move someplace else."

"I can understand why," said Emily. "But this is your home and—" Just then they heard a steady thud. "What's that?" They turned around and watched a basketball bounce down the stairs. "Where did that come from?"

Matt began to wail. "It was in our bedroom—in our closet!"

Emily, followed closely by the boys, sprinted up the stairs and into their room. The closet door was closed. She tried to open it, but the door barely moved. "Someone is inside the closet holding on to the doorknob," she told the boys. Emily yanked harder and ordered, "Whoever is in there, let go this instant!"

Suddenly, the door swung open, sending Emily reeling backward. She landed hard against the side of Matt's bed.

Now Emily was *really* angry. She scrambled to her feet and stood in front of the open closet. "The joking is over! Now get out here!" When she was met by silence, she cautiously stepped into the large, walk-in closet.

BANG! The door slammed shut behind her. She grabbed the doorknob, but it wouldn't turn. "Boys, I'm stuck in here. Let me out."

The brothers, feeling more scared than ever, hesitated before pulling on the doorknob. With Emily ramming her shoulder against the door, it grudgingly opened.

"See, Emily? This is not normal!" cried Matt.

"You're right about that," Emily said. "We'll talk to your parents when they come home. Maybe they can explain some of these—"

"Emily! Matt! Look!" Mike pointed to the doorway. The basketball was rolling slowly toward them.

"I don't suppose either one of you brought the ball back upstairs with you?" Emily asked hopefully. The wide-eyed boys gulped and shook their heads. "I didn't think so."

Before she could deal with the basketball, her attention was captured by a scraping sound on the wood floor. The boys' heavy chest of drawers was inching away from the wall—by itself! The three watched in horror as it squeaked and groaned. It moved about a foot before it stopped.

"Did you see that?" cried Mike.

Emily shoved the dresser back where it belonged. But the moment she stepped aside, it moved out again, this time stopping two feet from the wall. When she tried to push it back, it wouldn't budge. "Boys, help me."

But they remained rooted to their beds, too scared to move. The fear factor soared even higher moments later when their beds rose several inches off the floor. Then, like a ship on a stormy sea, the beds began rocking back and forth and pitching up and down. The petrified boys clutched their pillows as the violent shaking grew stronger.

Emily grabbed the boys by the wrists, yanked them off their bucking beds, and rushed them downstairs. They huddled in the family room, where Emily threw her arms around the shivering children. She was shaking too, but tried to stay composed for their sake.

"I'll call your parents," she said. But the top page of the notepad, where their phone number was written, was mysteriously torn off.

She quickly wrote a note that said "We're at my house—Emily," and left it on the kitchen counter. "Come on, boys, we're getting out of here!"

They ran to Emily's home five doors away. "Mom! Mom!" Emily blurted breathlessly. "The Curry house! It's possessed! Furniture moves by itself! Things fly through the air! It's awful!"

Bewildered, her mother asked, "Are you joking?"

"Look at me, Mom," barked Emily, still trembling. "Do I look like I'm joking? We're all scared out of our wits!"

"I don't understand, but I'll call the police." Mrs. Templeton dialed 911 and said, "We think there are intruders at the Curry house at 5692 Loblolly Lane."

Mrs. Templeton, Emily, and the boys met the police outside the Curry house. When Emily revealed what had happened, they stared at her suspiciously. Seeing the doubt in their faces, Mike maintained, "It really happened just like she said."

One of the officers mumbled something under his breath and then walked into the house with his partner. They found Legos scattered on the floor in the family room and noticed the boys' beds were at odd angles. The dresser stood in the middle of the bedroom.

"See?" said Emily as she followed the police inside. "The furniture moved by itself."

"You don't think someone could have done this?" asked the officer. "Like maybe the boys or one of their friends?"

"But the boys and I saw the furniture move on its own!" she insisted.

After further questioning and a check around the house, the police told Mrs. Templeton there was nothing they could do. "We see no sign of a break-in here," the officer said. "Has your daughter ever made up any stories?"

"Certainly not!" Mrs. Templeton scoffed. "How dare you insult my daughter like that!"

As the policemen headed out, everyone heard loud banging noises. "It's coming from upstairs!" Emily yelled.

The police bolted into the house and skidded to a stop in the doorway of the boys' room. "Do you see what I see?" the awed officer asked his partner.

"I was hoping my eyes were playing tricks on me," the partner replied. "But I guess they're not."

The lid to the boys' large toy chest was furiously opening and closing on its own. Finally, it broke off and fell to the floor. Seconds later, a toy spaceship flew out and crashed against the desk. A rubber ball shot out and ricocheted off the ceiling and wall. Then a box of checkers floated two feet above the chest before flipping over and spilling the checkers all over the floor.

In another corner of the room, miniature race cars on a figure-eight track suddenly came to life. They sped around the course so fast that they flew off the track and slammed into the side of the dresser. Meanwhile, action figures tumbled out of the toy chest like bees fleeing their hive.

Everyone was so shocked, they couldn't say a word. Finally, one of the officers broke the silence. "Uh, Dave, I'll let you write up the report on this one," he told his partner.

When the Currys came home, they were overwhelmed by the chilling accounts from their children. Then they were questioned by the officers, while Emily, her mother, and the boys listened.

"We've heard strange noises ever since we moved in," said Mr. Curry. "They usually came from the boys' room, so we assumed the boys were making them."

"The boys kept insisting they weren't responsible," recalled Mrs. Curry. "Then we noticed furniture had been moved, and toys ended up in places where they shouldn't be. We're at a loss to explain what's happening."

"I know what's happening," claimed Mike. "This house is haunted! I don't want to live here anymore. Can we move, please?"

Mrs. Curry shook her head helplessly. "I don't know what to do."

Emily's mother stepped forward. "I read in the paper last week about a group that investigates paranormal incidents. Maybe they can get to the bottom of this."

"It's worth a try," said Mr. Curry. "Anything is better than living like this."

Florence Imus of the Paranormal Research Society arrived at the Curry home two days later. She questioned the entire family and Emily too. Throughout the three hours that she was there, nothing out of the ordinary happened. In fact, there hadn't been any incidents since that frighteningly wild Saturday night.

"Emily, would you be kind enough to take the boys into the family room," said Florence. "I need to talk to Mr. and Mrs. Curry in private."

While Emily and the boys played cards using the deck that had no aces, Florence spoke softly but earnestly to the Currys. "I'll be frank with you. I definitely think a poltergeist is behind all this trouble. The moment I walked into your sons' bedroom, I felt the presence of a spiteful spirit. I want to try to communicate with it and find out why it is harassing Michael and Matthew—and Emily too."

"Exactly what is a poltergeist?" asked Mrs. Curry.

"It's a wicked spirit that moves objects, causes noises, and creates physical disturbances. It comes from the German words *poltern*, which means 'to knock,' and *geist*, which means 'spirit.' Reports of poltergeists date back to ancient Roman times and have been reported in all cultures through the centuries. Poltergeist activity usually starts and stops suddenly and rarely lasts longer than a few months. It almost always occurs when a particular person or persons are at home. In most cases, they are unknowingly triggering the poltergeist activity by their mere presence. It seems the poltergeist in this house is picking on your sons. My job is to figure out why and how to end this activity."

A loud bang in the boys' bedroom sent everyone charging upstairs. The poltergeist had thrown the desk chair ten feet across the room. The chair had splintered against the far wall, leaving a huge gouge.

"I was hoping to come back tomorrow to pick up any psychic impressions about the spirit," said Florence. "But perhaps I better try now. Everyone, please go downstairs and leave me alone in the room."

A half hour later, Florence entered the family

room, where Emily and the Currys were watching television. Mr. Curry stood up. "Well? Any luck?"

"I think so," Florence replied. "It seems this house has had a spirit for some time. I don't know who this person was, except I sense it was an older, crotchety man who couldn't stand kids. The letter *E* sticks in my mind."

"Mr. Enfield!" blurted Emily. "He used to live here. He was a mean old man. Nobody liked him, and he sure didn't like anybody."

"But he didn't die here," Mrs. Templeton pointed out. "He's not even dead as far as I know. He and his wife moved to Arizona after they sold the house to us."

"I think this spirit is older than the previous owner," said Florence.

"Mr. Enfield's father lived here with them for several years," said Emily. "I never saw him. I heard he was sick and in bed all the time. He died a couple of years ago. Could he be the spirit?"

"Very possibly," said Florence. "Apparently, this spirit still thinks of this house as his own. He's upset with the noise and activity because he dislikes kids. That's why he's been doing all these terrible things to Matthew and Mike. He even took out some of his malice on Emily."

"How do we get this ghost to leave?" asked Mrs. Curry.

"I made it clear to him that this was no longer his house—that he has not been invited to stay and needs to get out for good," Florence explained. "Whether or not he'll go right away, I can't say. But I feel confident he will leave soon."

"How can you be so sure?" asked Mrs. Curry.

Florence raised her eyebrows and grinned. "If a person can't stand noisy kids, what would he do if the children got wild and crazy? He leaves in search of peace and quiet." She turned to Mike and Matthew. "Boys, how would you like to have a screaming, jumping, free-for-all pillow fight?"

"Yeah!"

"And, Emily, how about joining them in their room? Make lots of noise and have a great time."

For the next half hour, Emily and the boys whomped each other with pillows, waged a Nerf-ball war, and hollered themselves hoarse. Sweaty and tired, they finally collapsed on the floor in a happy heap.

The Currys never had a problem with the poltergeist again. Unfortunately, Emily sometimes had a problem baby-sitting for the Curry boys. They claimed they needed to act wild and crazy—to keep the poltergeist away for good.

THE RUNAWAYS

Lakeisha Skidmore looked in on Dante Sifford to make sure the infant was sleeping peacefully in his crib. He had flipped onto his stomach, so she tenderly turned him over on his back, like his mother had instructed her to do.

As the fourteen-year-old sitter left the nursery and walked past the cellar door, she was startled to hear the rattling of chains and the tinkling of bells. She pressed her ear against the door. The rattling and tinkling gave way to the sound of sawing metal.

Is somebody down there? she wondered. *Maybe it's a burglar! Should I call 911?* Lakeisha tried to calm herself. *Wait. This is a very old house. Maybe it's just the furnace. If I call the police and it's nothing, the Siffords might get mad at me.*

Lakeisha was known in the neighborhood for her fearlessness. She opened the cellar door and caught a whiff of musty, cold air. Peering into the darkness, she bellowed in her strongest voice, "Who's down there?"

She heard nothing but the odd sounds of sawing metal and an occasional tinkling and rattling. She flicked on the light and looked again. The noise continued, but clearly no one was down there. *It must be the furnace,* she told herself.

She was wrong. Dead wrong.

After closing the cellar door, Lakeisha, who was sitting for Dante for the first time, couldn't help snooping around the old house. Donnell Sifford, an architect, and his wife, Nicole, had restored the 165-year-old three-story home into a showplace. Lakeisha poked her head in all the rooms, including Donnell's office on the top floor.

After returning to the main floor, she heard the strange tinkling and rattling coming from the cellar again. *I don't think it's the furnace. I wonder what it is. Well, there's only one way to find out.*

Lakeisha flipped on the light and slowly walked down the cellar steps. Although the Siffords had done wonders fixing up the old house, they hadn't remodeled the basement. The bare walls showed the original stone and mortar foundation. Wires snaked across the open rafters. Bare bulbs cast an eerie glow onto boxes, old furniture, and rusty paint cans.

When she reached the bottom step, she could

plainly hear chains rattling. Curious, the sitter walked to the far end of the basement—and then froze in astonishment.

In the shadows she saw the faint images of two shirtless young black men in tattered pants. She knew the men weren't real because she could see almost right through them, like watching a store window reflection of passersby. "Oh, my gosh, they're ghosts!" Lakeisha whispered to herself.

The taller man had thick chains clamped around his ankles; the other wore an iron collar with steel prongs going up each side of his head. Bells tinkled at the end of the prongs.

Lakeisha tried to slip behind an old chest, but she stumbled, knocking over several stacked boxes. Despite the racket she made, the two men acted as if she wasn't even there. Relieved, Lakeisha crouched next to the chest and watched in awe as the bizarre scene unfolded.

The man in the iron collar was sawing the ankle irons off his companion. When he turned his back to Lakeisha, she cringed. A gruesome network of thick raised scars crisscrossed his sweaty back.

"Alleluia, brother," whispered the tall one. "We're almost free!"

"We're gettin' closer to heaven on earth, Renty."

"Blessed are the Hogans for lettin' us hide here. Once we get off my leg irons and your slave collar, we'll be leavin' for Springfield."

"And we'll keep on movin' all the way to

Canada—as free men! Say that word with me, Renty: Free! Free! Free!"

"Shush, Josiah. Slave hunters are crawlin' all over this town. If they find us, they'll haul us back to the plantation."

"They can try to catch me all they want. I'll run away again and again. I might as well be killed runnin' as die standin'."

The images of the two men slowly disappeared. The rattling, tinkling, and sawing continued for several more seconds before they too faded away.

The astounded baby-sitter stepped unsteadily from behind the chest and walked over to the spot where the men had been. *I've always believed in ghosts,* she told herself, *but I never thought I'd really see them. But who will believe me? I have no proof.* Lakeisha stretched out her arms, feeling the air, wondering if by chance she would touch one of the now invisible ghosts.

The baby started crying, so Lakeisha hurried to the nursery and picked him up. As she held him close to her, she swayed back and forth. She needed someone to talk to, someone who would listen without challenging her improbable story.

"Dante, I just saw two ghosts! Real ones! Two black men. I'm pretty sure they were slaves escaping on the Underground Railroad. Should I tell Mama or your parents? Nah. They might think I'm whacked out. But I can tell you."

Even though she knew Dante didn't understand a

word she was saying, Lakeisha kept chattering. No matter how brave or confident she thought she was, the ghostly images had left her feeling extremely uneasy. Hoping that talking out loud would calm her, Lakeisha rambled on about the Underground Railroad—a subject she recently had studied in her history class.

"Before the Civil War, people who were against slavery helped runaway slaves flee north to freedom. The slaves were smuggled in wagons in the middle of the night, and they hid in farmhouses and homes in the city. At night these slaves kept moving to other houses farther north until they were free. The escape route was known as the Underground Railroad.

"If I'm right, Dante, you're probably living in a place that was once a safe house on the Underground Railroad. This is so exciting! And very creepy! But if I say anything about this and I'm wrong, your parents won't ever hire me as your baby-sitter and Mama will fret that I've lost my mind."

During the following week, Lakeisha read all she could about the Underground Railroad and the harsh realities of slave life on a southern plantation. She learned that by the age of twelve, most slaves were toiling in the fields from sunrise to sunset. They ate a poor diet of corn and fatty salted meat.

On the plantation, slaves lived in cramped, leaky, disease-breeding one-room shacks, and each cabin was crammed with up to a dozen men, women, and children. Slaves of all ages were sold at auctions, where they were paraded in front of white shoppers who sometimes made them jump or dance to show their liveliness. Shoppers squeezed the slaves' muscles and examined their teeth to determine their health, as if they were buying cattle.

Lakeisha found one book that illustrated how slaves were punished. Her eyes locked on a picture of iron fetters—strong ankle bracelets attached to a chain. *That's exactly what Renty was wearing!* she thought. On the next page, she saw a drawing of a slave collar with prongs and bells. *Just like Josiah's!*

Owners who found it unpleasant to beat slaves hired slave breakers to torture them. The most common form of punishment was a whipping. Blows from a long rawhide whip could take the skin off the back of a stripped and spread-eagled offender. A standard punishment was fifteen to twenty lashes, but the number for serious offenses often ran into the hundreds. Seeing a picture of a sickening pattern of scars on a slave's back, Lakeisha thought, *Those are just like the marks I saw on Josiah.*

Runaway slaves assumed the Underground Railroad brought them to freedom in the northern states. But in 1850, the federal government passed the Fugitive Slave Law. The law permitted northern authorities to issue warrants for the arrest and return of fugitive slaves. As a result, professional slave hunters armed with warrants scoured northern cities and often raided suspected safe houses.

The more Lakeisha learned about the Underground Railroad, the more fascinated she became. One reason was that, according to her family history, she was the descendant of slaves, whose names had been lost over time.

When Lakeisha baby-sat for Dante the next time, she was sure she would see Renty and Josiah again. She waited with guarded anticipation for the sounds of the bells, chain, and saw. But she didn't hear them.

About eleven o'clock that night, after making sure Dante was asleep, Lakeisha went down to the cellar. She stood behind the chest and stared toward the wall where she had last seen the ghosts. Within a few minutes, the transparent images appeared. The slave collar and chains lay on the floor.

"Now that my shackles are off, Josiah, I feel so much lighter." Renty smiled.

"Me too. The dread I've felt my whole life is liftin' off my shoulders."

"Josiah," Renty whispered, "what do you suppose Canada is like?"

"Cold, brother, cold in the winter. But it makes you feel warm here"—Josiah tapped his heart—"because we'll be free men. Imagine workin' at a job that pays you in money and in dignity. No more whuppins and slave collars."

"No more slave drivers and slave auctions."

"No more bowin' our heads and lowerin' our gaze when we talk to a white man."

"What're you gonna do when you get to Canada, Josiah?"

"Build me a home, raise me a family. Open up a lumber store. There's lots of lumber up there. What about you?"

"Horses. You know how I love horses. Gonna start me a farm and breed fine thoroughbreds."

"Shush, Renty. Do you hear somethin'?"

"Sounds like shoutin' outside. Mr. Hogan is yellin' somethin'. I heard the word 'slave hunter.' Josiah, we gotta get outta here. The first place they'll look is in the cellar. Quick, upstairs to the attic!"

The fugitives scrambled to their feet. Pointing to the shackles and slave collar, Josiah said, "We can't leave 'em lyin' here. Hide 'em where Mr. Hogan showed us." They pulled out a stone from the wall and tossed the tools of punishment inside. The men shoved the stone back as their images faded away.

The sitter stood dumbfounded for several minutes until she heard Dante fussing. Hustling to the nursery, she thought, *Every time those ghosts show up, Dante senses it.*

"It's okay, Dante, I'll cuddle you. Don't cry." An old plantation song that her grandmother had taught her popped into Lakeisha's mind. She began singing: "When I was a little bitty baby, my momma would rock me in the cradle, in them old cotton fields back home . . ."

Lakeisha stopped when she heard loud footsteps pounding toward the top floor. Dante had fallen back to sleep, so she placed him in his crib and dashed upstairs to Donnell's office. She turned on the light and gazed at the faint images of Renty and Josiah crouched in the corner.

"They're comin' up the stairs, Josiah!" Renty whispered frantically.

Josiah looked out the window. "No sense jumpin' out. The place is crawlin' with slave hunters. Someone snitched on us. Let's pray that Mr. Hogan can keep 'em outta here. Lay low in the closet."

Lakeisha saw no closet. But the men acted like they were hiding in one. Moments later, unseen hands dragged them out.

"No! No!" squealed Renty. "This is Illinois. It's a free state and we're free men!"

Although Lakeisha could barely view the slaves, she couldn't see the slave hunters at all, only the results of their brutality.

Renty fell to his knees and covered his face with his hands as a whip slashed his cheek. Josiah keeled over, apparently from the impact of a violent kick or punch.

"I ain't goin' back," snarled Josiah. "It ain't gonna do you any good if I'm dead, and you ain't gonna do me any good if I'm captured." He lunged at his attackers but reeled backward as three bullets ripped into his chest. He staggered briefly, opened his eyes wide, and defiantly declared with his last breath, "I'm a free man!" Then he collapsed in a pool of blood.

The gunshots caused Renty to throw his hands up in the air before a sneer crossed his lips. "I choose death to slavery. I'll be free one way or the other!"

Then he charged toward his attackers. Two blasts from a gun lifted him off his feet. As he lurched toward the wall, he crowed, "I'm comin' with you, Josiah."

Renty tumbled beside his companion. Blood from the two men trickled onto the floor, forming a crimson X. Then their bodies vanished.

Too stunned to stand, Lakeisha crumpled onto the carpeted floor and wept uncontrollably. She curled up into a ball and continued to wail until she felt a strong hand grasp her shoulder.

It was Donnell Sifford. "Lakeisha, why are you crying? Why are you in my office?"

Weeping and shaking, the sitter tried to talk, but her sentences came out in clumps of soggy words: "Ghosts . . . two slaves . . . Underground Railroad . . . kept here . . . slave hunters . . . killed here . . ."

Donnell turned to Nicole and said, "I think this girl is having a nervous breakdown. We better call her mother. It's a good thing Dante slept through all this."

By the time her mother, Harriet, arrived, Lakeisha had regained control of her emotions. Trying to sound as grown-up as she could, Lakeisha told them everything that she had seen and heard in the cellar and in the office. She explained why she believed she had witnessed the murders of two fugitive slaves who had been trapped in the safe house.

"Mr. and Mrs. Sifford, I'm not insane," Lakeisha declared.

Harriet held her daughter's still-quivering hands and said comfortingly, "I believe you."

Donnell scratched his head and paced the living room. "I find this almost impossible to believe. Yet there is a ring of truth to what you say, Lakeisha."

"How so?"

"I've done research on the history of this house," he explained. "It *was* part of the Underground Railroad in the 1840s. Tell me, Lakeisha, who did you say was the owner of this house when you saw these so-called phantom slaves?"

"Mr. Hogan."

"I'll be right back." Donnell returned a minute later with a tattered ream of papers. He began thumbing through the pages. "This is called an abstract. It documents all the owners of the house since it was built in 1832." Donnell let out a low whistle of surprise. "Well, get a load of this! In 1838, the house was sold to a Mr. Theodore Hogan."

"See?" exclaimed Lakeisha. "See? I told you!"

"Hogan sold the place to Grady Kingston in 1851. Your story seems to be holding up."

"I was right about Mr. Hogan," said Lakeisha. "Why don't you believe the rest of what I said?"

"Because it's so fantastic—ghosts in my house," Donnell replied. "We've never heard or seen any ghosts here. Nothing strange has ever happened to us."

"Maybe not to you, but it has to me," said Lakeisha.

"If what Lakeisha says is true, we should be able to find the secret hideaway in the basement," said Nicole.

Moments later, Lakeisha led them to the basement wall where she saw the slaves store the tools of punishment. Donnell took a pick axe and chipped away at the mortar surrounding a large stone. Within minutes, he worked the stone free and gazed into the void.

"Incredible!" marveled Donnell. "It's a hidey-hole. Not quite big enough for a person, but big enough to hide evidence of a slave." He reached in and pulled out a rusty piece of curved metal. "This could be an old iron piece from a shackle!"

Lakeisha began shaking from relief. "Now do you believe me?"

"It's getting harder not to," Donnell admitted. "You said the slaves hid in a closet in my office before they were shot, right?"

"Yes. I know you don't have a closet, but that's what it looked like. After they were shot, their blood formed an X on the wood floor."

"Lakeisha, when we bought this house, there used to be a closet in my office," said Donnell. "We tore it out and put down a carpet because the wood floor was in such terrible shape."

"Did you notice the bloodstains before you carpeted the floor?" she asked.

"No, but I wasn't looking for them. I recall the floor had all kinds of stains and markings. Let's see if we can find the spot where the two slaves died."

In the office, Donnell pulled back the carpet until it was about five feet from the wall. For a long moment, he couldn't speak. "Lakeisha, now I believe everything," he finally said. He pointed to a brown X on the floor—the bloodstains from the runaway slaves.

Lakeisha placed her hands on the stain and began to cry. Etched in her mind was the tragic scene of the last breaths taken by two brave men who sought nothing more than their basic right to freedom.

"There's one thing I don't understand," said Donnell. "Why did these phantoms appear to you but not to us? We've lived here for over two years."

Part of the answer came a week later after the Siffords invited Klaus Jergens, a noted ghost hunter, to investigate. At Klaus's suggestion, Lakeisha went with him to the cellar. Moments later, they saw the faint images of the two fugitives huddled in the corner, trying to free themselves from the iron bonds of slavery.

The stunning scene played out exactly the way Lakeisha had seen it earlier. Watching it for the second time was even more difficult for her. "I feel so bad for them," she moaned. "I know what's coming." Then she broke down and sobbed.

When the images vanished, Lakeisha begged the ghost hunter not to force her to relive the slaves' deaths in Donnell's office. "You won't have to," Klaus assured her. "I understand this is very hard for you."

Lakeisha, her mother, the Siffords, and Klaus gathered at the dining-room table. "So, what can you tell us about our ghosts?" Nicole asked the investigator.

"They are not ghosts," Klaus announced to everyone's surprise. "What Lakeisha witnessed are psychic imprints left behind by the deaths of Renty and Josiah."

"We don't understand," said Donnell.

"Psychic imprints are like supernatural videos of a profound event in someone's life," Klaus explained. "In this case, the imprints were of the last few minutes of the lives of Renty and Josiah.

"Some experts in my field believe that each one of us has an energy field that leaves behind an unseen image of important moments in our life at the spot where these moments happened. These images remain long after we die. Under rare circumstances, other people—usually a psychic or someone connected to the person who died—will see one or more of these imprints. The scenes from psychic imprints remain in the same spot and are repeated over and over.

"These imprints are always identical and the details never change. It's the same as watching a video for the second or third time. It will always be the same.

"Lakeisha, if what you had seen were really ghosts, they could have talked to you or responded to you in some way. Ghosts have, in an odd sort of way, a life of their own. Psychic imprints don't."

Lakeisha pondered Klaus's explanation for several minutes before saying, "Why did I see Renty's and Josiah's psychic imprints? I don't know them and I'm not psychic."

"Maybe you are psychic and don't know it," Klaus answered. "And maybe you do have a connection with Renty and Josiah. Perhaps they are related to you."

"That very well could be true," said Harriet. "I've spent years working on our family tree, and I know some of our ancestors were slaves. But finding names from before the Civil War is extremely difficult. Census reports didn't list African Americans by last names before 1870. I guess we'll never know who Renty and Josiah were."

When Lakeisha left the Siffords, she knew she could never baby-sit in that house again. She never wanted to go through the gut-wrenching experience of seeing and hearing Renty and Josiah's final terror-stricken minutes. However, she couldn't forget the strong possibility that she somehow was linked to the fugitives.

"Mama, let's do another search of our family's past and look for Renty and Josiah," she suggested.

"It's almost an impossible task to find our slave ancestors, Lakeisha," Harriet told her.

"We have to try, Mama. I need to know."

The earliest known ancestor was Lakeisha's great-great-great grandfather Toby Skidmore, a Tennessee sharecropper who died in 1878 around the age of forty.

During her research, Lakeisha learned that slaves had often taken the last name of their most recent owner and that the slaves' descendants usually stayed in the same general area. Sifting through the records, she and her mother identified three plantation owners whose last name was Skidmore.

"Mama, when would the names of slaves be put on an official record?" Lakeisha asked.

"Most likely when the owner died and left a will and a copy of his estate inventory—a list of his possessions," Harriet replied.

"So we need to find out when the three plantation owners named Skidmore died and look for their records. Hopefully, they'll list the names of their slaves. If we can find Toby's name in one of the records, it could lead us to Toby's—and our—relatives. And just maybe our relatives will include Renty and Josiah."

During the summer, mother and daughter went to Tennessee, where their ancestors on both sides of the family had come from. In libraries and courthouses, they pored over wills and estate settlements that often mentioned slaves by name and age. After hitting a dead end with the first two Skidmores, Lakeisha found a copy of the will of plantation owner Chandler Skidmore, who had died in 1849.

"Oh, please be the one," she prayed. Her heart pounding with suspense, Lakeisha read through the holdings: cattle, hogs, buggies, and twelve slaves. She closed her eyes as she turned the page. "Please list their names. Please!" She opened her eyes and saw a neatly printed list of slaves' names and ages.

Swiftly scanning the list, Lakeisha let out a whoop that shattered the quiet of the hushed library reading room. "Mama! Mama!" Lakeisha squealed, leaping up and dancing around the table. "Look! Look!" Among the slaves whose names were penned on the copy of Chandler Skidmore's list of holdings were three brothers:

> Toby, 11
> Renty, 19
> Josiah, 21

Lakeisha caught her mother in a joyous, tearful bear hug. "Mama, we found them! We found Renty and Josiah! They're family!"

THE PHANTOM FIDDLER

As Sara Mahoney tucked six-year-old Tiffany Ferguson under her Barbie sheets, the pixie-faced little girl looked up and asked, "Sara, do you believe in ghosts?"

Sara flicked her brown bangs, plopped down on the edge of the bed, and mulled over the unexpected question. "I've never seen one," replied the twelve-year-old baby-sitter, "but I guess spirits exist. Why? Do you believe in ghosts?"

Tiffany hesitated for several seconds before answering, "Mommy says there are no such things as ghosts."

"Then maybe you should believe your mommy," said Sara, thinking that further talk of ghosts might scare the little girl. "Good night, Tiffany. I'll leave the door open and the hall light on."

Sara had barely reached the door, when Tiffany

asked, "Do you have to be special to see ghosts? Like do some people see them and some people don't?"

"Tiffany, we're all special. Now get to sleep."

Sara wouldn't have been so quick to blow off talk about ghosts had she known the attic held a tragic secret.

Tim and Bailey Ferguson lived in one of the most unique houses in the neighborhood. The main section had been a small two-story house made of limestone in the 1870s. It had a living and dining area downstairs and two small bedrooms upstairs. In the 1980s, the Fergusons bought the place and added a new one-story wing of cedar, stone, and glass. The addition contained a spacious, modern kitchen, plus a master bedroom and bath.

Tiffany slept in the old section of the house in a room far different from her friends'. Her bedroom featured the original rough limestone walls that revealed a history of the many people who had slept there. These people had left their marks by carving their initials and symbols on the stone walls. The yellow pine floor also had its share of scratchings, and creaked even under Tiffany's light weight.

After she'd tucked Tiffany into bed, Sara headed downstairs to the living room. She was curled up on the couch, thumbing through the latest issue of *Sassy* magazine, when she heard the faint tune of a fiddle. The music was light and gay, the kind played at square dances.

Where's that coming from? she wondered. Sara opened the front door and stepped out into the warm summer night. All was quiet. She went back inside and walked around the house. *Maybe the Fergusons forgot to turn off the radio or TV in their room,* Sara thought. She peeked into their bedroom, but neither was on.

Sara could hear the faint fiddle music as she climbed the stairs. But it stopped when she entered Tiffany's room. The little girl was asleep, and her tape player was off. *She couldn't have turned off a tape and then jumped into bed without me hearing her,* Sara thought.

She flicked her bangs again in confusion and then went back downstairs. About an hour later, she heard the fiddle again. *Boy, that's starting to bug me,* Sara thought. It wasn't the music that bothered her—it was not knowing its source. *I'm just going to ignore it.*

A few moments later, she heard the padding of bare feet on the stairs. Tiffany, her eyes squinting in the light, made her way into the living room. "I can't sleep. He's playing his fiddle again."

"Who is?"

"That boy Jacob," Tiffany answered with a yawn.

"A boy?" Sara asked in surprise. "Where?"

"In my room."

"What! You stay here!"

Sara charged upstairs and bolted into Tiffany's room, but saw no boy, even after she searched under the bed and in the closet. Only then did she realize that the fiddling had stopped. After checking out the other bedroom on the second floor, a puzzled

Sara returned to the living room downstairs.

Seeing Tiffany asleep on the couch, Sara smiled. The little girl had been dreaming, that's all. Sara carried Tiffany back to her bed. But when she returned to the couch, Sara had a strange thought. *If Tiffany was dreaming about a boy fiddling, then how come I heard a fiddle playing?*

A half hour later, Tim and Bailey Ferguson returned home. "How was Tiffany?" asked Bailey.

"Fine, as always," Sara replied. "She got up a little while ago because she said a boy was playing the fiddle in her room. Of course, no one was there."

"She must have been dreaming."

"Yes, but the funny thing is that I heard fiddle music too. Do you know who it could have been?"

Bailey turned to her husband. "Maybe the Bergers. They're always playing their music too loud," she said.

"Yeah, that must have been it," said Sara, knowing full well the fiddle playing hadn't been from the neighbors across the street.

Sara had forgotten about Tiffany's imaginary fiddler by the following Saturday night, when she baby-sat at the Fergusons' again. Tiffany didn't mention the boy all evening.

At bedtime, Tiffany slipped into her Barbie pajamas and selected a new book for Sara to read out loud. "Mommy got this for me today. You'll be the first to read it to me."

After Tiffany snuggled into bed, Sara pulled up a

chair and opened the book, *The Village Melody*. It was a fable about how music can sound sweet to one person but be absolutely annoying to another. In the story, the mayor ran a contest seeking the best tune for the village band to play. The townspeople took turns playing their original songs on a wide variety of instruments, but, unfortunately, no one liked anyone else's music. The mayor was about to give up when someone suggested that they all play at the same time. Magically, all their music and instruments blended in perfect harmony. By working together they had created the village melody.

While reading the book to Tiffany, Sara did her best to imitate the sounds of the various musical instruments. When she turned to the page about the fiddler, Sara pretended to play the fiddle. She stood up on the chair and bobbed her head while playing "air fiddle" with an empty shoe box and a ruler.

Tiffany giggled and clapped. "You play just like Jacob does—only he has a real fiddle and plays real music."

Sara got down off the chair and sat on the bed next to Tiffany. "Who is Jacob?"

"It's a secret."

"Is he the boy you saw last Saturday night?"

Tiffany nodded. "I've seen him lots of times."

"When?"

"At night. Always at night when Mommy and Daddy are asleep. I am too sometimes. He wakes me up with his fiddle playing."

"And he comes right into your room?"

"Uh-huh. He stands over in the corner and plays and plays. Not too loud. Sometimes he smiles and sometimes he looks very sad."

"Where does he come from? How does he get in here?"

"I don't know, Sara. Jacob just shows up."

"Does he say anything to you?"

"Just things like 'Hi' and 'Let me play for you.'"

"What's he look like?"

"Well, he has a blue shirt and dark pants and no shoes. He's bigger than me but shorter than you. He's maybe in fourth or fifth grade. His hair is long and shaggy."

"What does he do when he finishes playing?"

"He, um, disappears."

"You mean out the door?"

"No, he fades away."

Sara had two younger brothers, and she knew that little kids often had imaginary playmates. Still, that couldn't explain why she too had heard the fiddle.

"Do you think Jacob is a ghost?" asked Tiffany.

Don't you dare say yes, Sara thought. *The next thing you know, Tiffany will tell her mother that you believe in ghosts and then you'll get in trouble. I can just hear Mrs. Ferguson say, "What crazy ideas are you putting in my child's head?"*

"Tiffany, I don't know who he is. He's probably a very nice imaginary friend."

"He's not make-believe. He's real—a real ghost."

"Have you told your mommy and daddy about Jacob?"

Tiffany shook her head. "It's a secret—just you and me know."

"Why is it a secret?"

"Jacob told me not to tell. He likes me and wants to play just for me. He says grown-ups wouldn't understand."

"Will you come get me the next time he plays?" Sara asked.

"Okay."

"Great. Night-night," said Sara.

Downstairs, Sara stretched out on the couch with a magazine. But she soon found herself rereading the same paragraph. Her mind kept drifting to thoughts of this Jacob—whoever he was. *He's got to be imaginary. There's no way a boy could sneak into her room.*

A tiny freezing-cold hand touched her shoulder. Sara jumped to her feet with a yelp. "Tiffany!"

The sleepy-eyed girl mumbled, "He's here."

"Jacob is in your room?"

"Uh-huh."

Once again, Sara detected the faint sounds of a fiddle playing that haunting music. She scampered up the steps. This time, the music grew louder and more lively the closer she came to Tiffany's bedroom.

Sara bounded into the room and gasped. Standing in the corner, exactly as Tiffany had described, was a barefoot boy about ten years old playing a fiddle. His head bobbing in sync to a delightfully catchy tune, the boy skillfully moved the bow across the strings with short, sharp strokes. He flashed a toothy grin.

It was shocking enough to see a strange young fiddler in Tiffany's room. But far more startling for Sara was that she literally could see right through him.

Sara's legs were about to buckle from the sight of something so incredible. She grabbed the doorknob for support. The spellbound sitter watched in utter amazement while the boy fiddled with great passion and joy. But soon he slowly faded away. The music did too, lingering several seconds after he had disappeared.

"See, I told you," said Tiffany, tugging at Sara's T-shirt.

"I—I d-don't know what to say . . . or what to th-think," Sara stammered. She stumbled over to the bed and clutched Tiffany's teddy bear. "The boy definitely looked like a ghost."

"He *is* a ghost, silly," said Tiffany. "We can see him. That means you and I are special."

"Special, yeah," mumbled Sara, her mind still trying to make sense of what she had just seen.

"Jacob isn't make-believe, Sara."

"You're right about that." Sara held the teddy bear even tighter. "Did he say anything to you when you first saw him tonight?"

"He said he wanted to play for me. I asked him if

it was okay if you came up to hear him because you're a special person. He said it would be all right."

"I wonder who he is and why he plays the fiddle. Maybe he lived here a long time ago. This is an old house." Sara glanced at several of the carvings on the stone wall by the bed: a triangle, TSG, an outline of a dog, JW, interlocking circles, 2–22–22, HI!, and MM+CR inside a crude heart. *It sure would be cool to know who carved these things,* she thought. *Could Jacob have been one of them? The initials JW could stand for Jacob somebody.* Sara trembled with nervous excitement over her ghostly encounter.

Tiffany yawned. "I'm tired." She climbed into bed and squirmed under her sheets.

Sara sat on the bed. *How can Tiffany be so calm? Look at me. I'm still shivering. We just saw an honest to goodness ghost!* "Tiffany, do you mind if I hold on to your teddy bear?"

"Sure. He's good to hug when you're scared."

Sara scooted down and lay beside Tiffany. "I'll stay here with you until your parents come home."

Soon the sitter's uneasiness over seeing Jacob's ghost gave way to curiosity. Sara wanted to see him again, find out who he was, where he was from, and why he was haunting this house—and Tiffany's room in particular.

She looked at her watch. The Fergusons weren't due home for another two hours. She stroked Tiffany's head until the little girl fell asleep. Then Sara whispered, "Jacob, if you can hear me, please come back and talk to me. I've got a zillion questions for you." She closed her eyes, waiting and hoping to see the boy fiddler again.

Kirby Wheeler stroked his beard. Sweat from his shirtless chest soaked through his grimy coveralls. "It's hotter than a black mare's rump at high noon," he told his wife, Martha.

"Sure is." Decked out in a wide-brimmed hat, Martha flapped her long red dress. "I need to get air on my legs."

The couple stood outside their small limestone house and watched their barefoot son, Jacob, chase a rooster. They were waiting for the arrival of the Hales, Martha's folks from back east, who hadn't seen the family for five years.

When the Hales finally rode up in their wagon, Jacob ran to give his grandparents big hugs and kisses, then eagerly helped them unload. One of the items he lifted out of the wagon was a stringed wooden instrument. "Granddaddy, what's this?"

"That's my fiddle, Jacob."

"What's it do?"

"It makes people happy. Here, let me show you." The old man placed the fiddle under his chin and played a quick toe-tapping tune.

Jacob pranced around to the music. "I never heard of such a thing," he chuckled. "It's mighty fine."

"The Hales are great fiddlers," said Grandpa.

"When your mama was still living with us, she could fiddle the wool right off a lamb. So could her sisters." Nodding proudly to his daughter, Grandpa said, "Isn't that right, Martha?"

Martha blushed. "I guess."

"Can I try it, Granddaddy?"

"Certainly, Jacob." Grandpa handed the fiddle to his grandson and showed him how to hold the instrument and handle the bow.

But Jacob's father stopped him before he could try to play a note. "Jacob!" he thundered. "Put that darn fool thing down! I don't ever want any of that fiddling in my house."

"But, Daddy, I'm not in our house. I'm outside."

His eyes flashing with anger, Kirby turned to the Hales and hissed, "See what that fiddle has brought? Now my son is sassing back to me. Fiddling makes people say and do all sorts of crazy things and leads a body away from the things he ought to be doing." Turning to his son, he warned, "Jacob, you're never to play that instrument again. If you do, you will feel the full brunt of my wrath."

Martha wanted to come to her son's aid, but she held her tongue. She and Jacob were both afraid of Kirby. Even though he was an otherwise decent and honorable man, he was strict—and known to have a fiery temper.

The next day, while Kirby was in town to buy supplies, Grandpa Hale boldly played the fiddle for Jacob. Then the old man handed the instrument to

Martha and urged her to play it. She caressed the curves of the wooden instrument from its neck, down its back, to its sidepieces. After fondling the fingerboard, she picked up the bow and gently guided it across the strings.

Her eyes glistened as she fondly remembered the tunes she used to play when she was growing up. "I haven't fiddled in over a dozen years. Kirby would raise holy terror with me if he knew what I was about to do," she said with a devilish grin. She took a deep breath and then launched into the lively song "Turkey in the Straw."

Martha's parents linked arms and danced a little jig while Jacob clapped and hopped around. With each stroke she made across the strings, Martha's fiddling grew stronger and more spirited. "Oh, how I miss this music. If only Kirby weren't so dead set against it."

"Tell you what," said Grandpa Hale, catching his breath and wiping the sweat off his face. "Why don't you keep the fiddle. Hide it in a safe spot. Then, whenever Kirby is gone, you and Jacob could play it."

"Well, I guess it wouldn't hurt anything," said Martha. "It's not like we're doing anything wrong." She and Jacob hid the fiddle under a loose floorboard in the attic, right below a large stain in the ceiling that, ironically, had the hourglass shape of a fiddle's body.

Kirby often left home for several days at a time to work as a stonemason in nearby towns. His trips allowed Martha the opportunity to teach Jacob how to play the fiddle. The boy was a quick study and soon became almost as good a fiddler as his mother.

One sweltering summer day, Kirby headed to Pikeville, a town in the next county, for a job that would take about a week to complete. That evening, Jacob went up into the attic, brought down the fiddle, and played for his mother. Every once in a while, she fiddled a new tune and turned the instrument back over to her son to copy. The two had such a good time, they played late into the night.

Meanwhile, when Kirby arrived in Pikeville, he learned that the job he was supposed to do had been given to someone else. Furious, he hopped into his wagon and headed back home. When the tired and still fuming man pulled up to the house late that same night, he wondered why the lamp was still burning. As he neared the door, he learned why.

A gay melody danced out the open window. But rather than lighten his heart, it darkened his already foul mood. In a rage, Kirby flung open the door and confronted his startled son and wife. "Jacob Wheeler, how dare you!" he bellowed, snatching the fiddle from Jacob's hands. Yanking a knife from his belt, Kirby angrily sliced the strings from the fiddle. Then he tied it to a nail near the mantel and thundered, "There hangs the instrument of evil as a reminder to all who would not obey." He swiped the bow from Jacob's trembling hands, snapped it over his knees, and threw it at his son.

Jacob picked up the broken bow, never once taking his eyes off his father's boiling mad face.

"I warned you, Jacob, never to touch a fiddle. Now you must face the consequences." Kirby grabbed the boy by the wrist and dragged him upstairs. Kirby then leaned a handmade ladder against the wall. He climbed up and unfastened a hinged door in the ceiling that opened to the attic. He climbed down the ladder and ordered Jacob, "Get up there!"

"In the attic?"

"Yes! I want you to spend time in solitary, thinking about how you disobeyed me."

"How long do I have to stay there?"

"Until I say! Now move!"

Reluctantly, Jacob, still clutching the broken bow, climbed into the dark, windowless room. "It's hot and stuffy up here, Daddy. It's hard to breathe."

"Good! Maybe this will teach you a lesson!" Kirby slammed the door and bolted it with a chunk of wood.

Martha tearfully begged Kirby to go easy on Jacob. "It's not his fault," she said. "I encouraged him to play."

"Woman," he hissed, "I will not speak to you for fear I will utter such vile words that your ears would smolder. Stay away from me, keep quiet, and don't go near Jacob's room!"

The night was insufferably hot and sticky with no hint of a breeze. The thick, calm air was almost impossible to breathe. Martha tossed and turned and fretfully waited for her husband to fall asleep. Then she crept over to Jacob's room, hoping to get him out of the attic. But the wooden floor betrayed her when it creaked under her feet, waking Kirby up. In a flash, he barged into Jacob's room and yanked Martha back to bed. "You are pushing me past the limit of my restraint," he snapped. "Do as I say or I will punish you too."

The next morning, Kirby, satisfied that his son had learned his lesson, opened the attic door. "All right, son, you can come down," he said. But Kirby was greeted by silence. "Did you hear me? Get down here!"

His anger rising by the second, Kirby peered into the attic. Jacob was slumped in the far corner where the roof met the floor, just below the fiddle-shaped stain. "Jacob! Wake up! Jacob!" His son didn't stir.

Kirby crawled over to him and began shaking him, but the boy didn't move. Kirby's fury gave way to concern. "Jacob! Jacob!" He placed his hand on the boy's heart, then neck, and wrist, but he felt no pulse.

Jacob was dead.

Cradling his limp son, Kirby let out a heart-wrenching wail that sent dust drifting down from the attic ceiling. When Martha saw what had happened to her only child, she screeched and fainted.

"Sara. Wake up, Sara." Bailey's soft voice brought a merciful end to Sara's dream.

"Oh, Mrs. Ferguson," mumbled Sara, slowly sitting up in Tiffany's bed. "I'm sorry I conked out. Tiffany had trouble sleeping, so I lay down with her and I guess I was tired—"

"It's all right, Sara. But are you all right?"

"What do you mean?"

"There are tears running down your face."

Sara lifted her hands to her face and felt wet cheeks. "I had a bad dream." She looked up at the ceiling and grimaced at the sight of the door to the attic. Then her eyes moved to the wall by the bed and focused in on the carved initials JW.

"JW," Sara whispered to herself. "Jacob Wheeler."

"Pardon, Sara?"

Sara wanted to tell her everything, but she was afraid Bailey wouldn't believe her. "Nothing, Mrs. Ferguson. Nothing at all."

Sara didn't fall asleep until the wee hours of the morning. She kept reliving her encounter with Jacob's ghost and her vivid dream. She was convinced that Jacob's spirit had haunted her dream so he could tell her what had happened to him.

The next week, Sara baby-sat for Tiffany again. The moment the Fergusons left, Sara eagerly asked, "Have you seen Jacob?"

"Uh-huh," Tiffany replied. "Last night he played."

"Did he say anything?"

"Just that you knew everything. He looked real sad."

When it was time for bed, Sara took Tiffany to her room and read her another story. But she couldn't manage her usual lively reading style.

"Is something wrong, Sara? You look sad."

Sara shook her head. "I'm sorry, honey. Everything is fine. Just fine." But Sara couldn't take her eyes off the attic door. She felt an odd urge to go up there.

About an hour after Tiffany had fallen asleep, Sara couldn't stand it any longer. *I have to go up in the attic,* she thought.

She brought a stepladder from the garage and quietly placed it in Tiffany's room under the attic door. Armed with a flashlight, Sara climbed the ladder and, with some effort, opened the balky, squeaky door. Tiffany stirred but didn't wake up. Dust rained from the attic ceiling, and Sara had to hold her nose to keep from sneezing.

She turned on the flashlight and poked her head above the opening. The attic was empty except for spiderwebs spread across the rafters.

There's nothing here. Get down before Tiffany wakes up. Don't go any further. But despite her own conscience warning her, Sara continued to climb the ladder until she'd boosted herself onto the floor of the attic. *You're going to get into so much trouble. What are you looking for?* Sara didn't know.

The heavy stifling air made her gag. She imagined what it must have been like for Jacob—a boy imprisoned by his father in a deadly chamber, groping in the darkness, gasping for air as the sweltering heat slowly, mercilessly sweated the life out of him.

Sara began to feel faint. *You need air! Get out of here now before you pass out!*

The flashlight dropped from her hand onto the attic floor. Struggling to keep from fainting, she turned around on her hands and knees. Then she stuck her head down the opening and gulped the cool breeze coming from the bedroom air conditioner.

Revived, Sara picked up the flashlight and began lowering herself down the ladder. Suddenly, the beam of her flashlight shone on a fiddle-shaped water stain where the roof met the attic floor.

That's the same stain I saw in my dream! That's where Jacob was lying when his dad found him. Jacob was right over there when he . . . when he . . . died. Sara felt sick to her stomach.

Then she saw a slender object poking up from a hole in the attic floor. *What's that below the stain?* Sara wondered. She crawled to the object. *It's a broken bow! Jacob's bow!*

Even though sweat trickled down her face, Sara felt a terrible chill. She grabbed the bow and left the attic.

When she reached the bottom of the ladder, she heard Tiffany say, "Sara, what are you doing?"

"I, um, heard a noise and I wanted to make sure everything was okay."

"You were looking for Jacob, weren't you?"

"Why do you say that?"

"Because I had a bad dream about him. He was stuck in the attic. He was crying and then he died." Noticing the broken bow in Sara's hand, Tiffany asked, "Is that Jacob's?"

Sara nodded. "I'll be right back and then we can talk about it." After putting the ladder and flashlight away, Sara returned to Tiffany's room. Jacob's ghost was there, playing a soft, somber tune for Tiffany.

He really doesn't belong here, Sara thought. *I mean, even friendly ghosts shouldn't be haunting people's houses. Maybe he would be happier elsewhere.*

Sara cleared her throat and spoke directly to the ghost. "I feel awful for what happened to you here, Jacob. You deserve to be happy. Maybe you should go to some other place, where ghosts are supposed to go. You shouldn't be hanging around a little girl's bedroom."

Tiffany began to whimper. "But I like him, Sara. Even if he does wake me up sometimes."

"You want him to stay?"

After Tiffany nodded vigorously, Sara turned to Jacob. "Do you want to keep playing for Tiffany?"

Jacob lowered his fiddle and stared at both of them. Then he broke out in that toothy grin of his, tucked the instrument under his chin, and launched into a merry tune.

THE PEST

Nick Alomar sat for six-year-old Roberto Perez only once. Everyone agreed that once was one time too many.

In fact, after what happened to Nick on that fateful night at the Perez residence, the thirteen-year-old boy swore he would never, ever baby-sit for anyone again. Especially for a family as weird as the Perezes.

Nick seldom baby-sat. But his mother roped him into the job because her new friend from yoga class, Vana Perez, needed a sitter. Nick said no—until he learned how much the Perezes were paying.

When Mrs. Perez picked Nick up, he immediately had a bad feeling about her. Flashing long dark purple fingernails that matched the color of her lipstick, Mrs. Perez shook his hand with both of hers. "Oh, I can feel your aura," she told him. "It's quite strong."

"Aura?"

"Yes, that's the energy field surrounding your body. If you take the time, you might be able to see and feel it on other people. Yours is particularly bright. Are you psychic?"

"Not that I know of," Nick replied. "Although I am pretty good at picking the winners of college football games. Does that count?"

"Possibly. My husband and I and our son, Roberto, are psychic."

"You mean you can predict the future?"

"No. It's more that we can understand things and see things that others might not. It's a gift."

Mrs. Perez pulled into the driveway of her stucco and wood Tudor-style house with its steeply angled roof. The moment Nick walked inside, he wished he hadn't agreed to baby-sit.

The atmosphere gave him the creeps. Dark, heavy antique furniture gave the rooms a dreary feeling. Sculptures of leering, hideous-looking creatures squatted in nooks and crannies. The walls were covered with drawings and paintings of faces twisted in fury and panic—expressions that Nick thought belonged in nightmares, not on canvas.

"This is Roberto," Mrs. Perez announced.

A frail-looking boy with curly black hair and large thick glasses stepped into the center hall. He held a book in his hand. A black T-shirt featuring the face of famed horror writer Edgar Allan Poe drooped over his skinny frame.

"Roberto, this is Nick," said Mrs. Perez. "He'll be sitting for you tonight."

Roberto muttered a halfhearted "Hi," then ambled back into the living room.

Roberto's father, who looked like an adult version of the boy, told Nick, "Help yourself to anything in the refrigerator or pantry. Carrot juice, rice cakes, trail mix, celery juice. We'll be back past the bewitching hour. Roberto, you be good for Nick. Good-bye."

After they left, Nick locked the front door. As he walked toward the living room, he was startled by a loud yowl. A dark blur leaped on his leg. Nick screamed. A black cat had sunk its claws through Nick's jeans and into the back of his calf.

"Get off me!" Nick squealed, trying to pry the hissing cat from his leg.

Roberto hurried to the rescue and pulled the cat away from the sitter. "What's the matter, Spooky?" Roberto cooed. "Did he step on you?"

"I didn't step on your cat," Nick protested. "I wasn't anywhere near him. He attacked me for no reason."

"Spooky doesn't hurt anyone, do you, Spooky?" said Roberto, cuddling his now-purring pet. The cat nuzzled sweetly under his chin. "That's the first time he's ever done anything like that."

"He came out of nowhere. If I accidentally scared him, I'm sorry, but I didn't see him." Nick tried to pet the cat but it spat at him. "Hopefully I'll get along better with you, Roberto. So, what would you like to do?"

Roberto handed him a thick book called *Day of the Dead*. Pointing to a page showing a sketch of a dead body in a coffin, the boy asked, "Would you read this to me?"

"Whoa, aren't you a little young for this?"

"No, Mom reads me stuff like this all the time."

"Well, if you're sure."

They sat on the couch and Nick began reading. "The Day of the Dead is a special holiday each year to honor the dead. People throw parties, make feasts, cook special foods, sing songs about the dead, and even have parades.

"In Japan, the Feast of Lanterns is celebrated between July thirteenth and sixteenth. It is believed that the spirits of the dead come home during this time. They are entertained with food and—"

WHAM! The front door flew open, slamming hard against the wall. Nick jumped up, threw down the book, and ran to the center hall.

That's strange, he thought, closing the door. *It's not windy outside. Even if it was, I know I bolted the door. But now it's unlocked! Roberto couldn't have unlocked it. He hasn't been out of my sight.*

"Nick, will you read some more from *Day of the Dead*?"

"Can't we try something else, like *James and the Giant Peach*?"

"No, I want this!"

Returning to the living room, Nick read, "In China, the Hungry Ghost Festival takes place in the fall and lasts for two weeks. People prepare offerings of food for those ghosts who have no living relatives to take care of them, and therefore are hungry. The ghosts are symbolized by lotus flower lamps that are carried through the streets, and small boats with candles that are floated in streams—"

CRRREEEAAAKKK!

"It's the door," Nick fretted. "How could it possibly open again?"

"I thought you locked it."

"I did."

"Oh, no, where's Spooky?" Roberto whined. "He's not supposed to go outside. The neighbor's dogs will chase him." The boy's eyes filled with tears. "You should've made sure the door was locked, Nick. Now he's gone."

"I *did* lock the door. I don't know how it got open. Come on, let's go look for your cat."

The moment they stepped outside, the door banged shut behind them. Nick tried to open it, but somehow it was locked—and so were the windows. "I don't suppose you have a key hidden anywhere outside."

Roberto shook his head.

"Do you know if a neighbor has a key?"

Roberto shook his head again.

"We're not getting off to a good start here, are we, Roberto?"

Roberto wiped his tears with his Poe T-shirt. "I want Spooky. And I want to get back in my house."

"It's going to be dark in another ten minutes. Let's try to find your cat, and then we'll figure out a way to get inside."

They searched the area without success. "He'll come back," said Nick. "Cats always do." *Especially the mean ones,* he thought.

"How are we going to get back inside?" Roberto asked. As he spoke, the door mysteriously swung open.

"Yippee!" Roberto cheered. "It wasn't locked after all!"

"Yes, it was," declared Nick, "but I'm not even going to try to figure out how this all happened."

Once inside, Roberto said in a know-it-all voice, "Here, let me lock it." He closed the door, turned the bolt, and shook the doorknob. "There, it won't open now. I'm thirsty. I want some carrot juice."

Nick made a sour face. As he took out the jug of carrot juice from the refrigerator, he looked for something else to drink. "Don't you have anything good in here like Yoo Hoo or root beer?"

"Natural stuff is better for you," said Roberto.

"Not for my taste buds," Nick muttered.

Nick opened the cabinet to get a glass—and one tumbled out and crashed into dozens of tiny slivers on the tile floor. "Did you see that? The glass fell by itself."

"No, it didn't," said Roberto. "You dropped it."

"I didn't even touch it!"

After cleaning up the broken pieces, Nick reached

for another glass. The cabinet door slammed on his hand. "Ow!" howled Nick, opening the door and rubbing his sore fingers. He glared at Roberto. "What's going on here?"

Roberto shrugged. "That's the first time I've seen that happen."

Nick opened the cabinet door and held it while he took out a glass. As he put it on the counter next to the jug of carrot juice, the puzzled sitter watched the cabinet door shut on its own again.

As he wondered what was going on, Nick realized his feet were beginning to feel wet. "Oh, man," he griped. "Now look." The jug had tipped over, and a steady stream of carrot juice was cascading off the counter onto his tennis shoes. Getting increasingly annoyed, Nick stared at Roberto.

"Don't look at me," said Roberto. "I didn't do it."

"Oh, the jug just happened to spill on its own?"

While cleaning up the mess, Nick thought, *Why did I agree to take this job? It's going from bad to worse. No, it's going from weird to bizarre.* "Do me a favor, Roberto. Next time you want something in the kitchen, get it yourself."

A few minutes later, Nick headed for the bathroom. As he reached the door, he heard a click and discovered it was locked. "Roberto, are you in there?" asked Nick, knocking on the door. "Roberto?"

"What do you want?" replied the little boy, walking up behind him in the hallway.

"Roberto, what are you doing out here?"

"You called me."

"I heard someone lock the bathroom door, so I assumed you were inside. I can hear the water running too."

"If I'm out here, then who's inside?"

"You tell me, Roberto. Is there someone else in this house who I should know about?"

"Not really."

"What do you mean, 'not really'?"

Suddenly, they heard a click. Nick turned the doorknob and opened the door. As he stepped inside, a black blur sailed out of the sink—straight toward him! "Yikes!" Nick yelled, dodging out of the way.

"Spooky!" exclaimed Roberto. "What are you doing in the bathroom?" He picked up his cat and hugged him.

Hot water was running in the sink, filling the bathroom with steam. When Nick tried to shut off the tap, the handle came off and hot water spewed onto his hand. "Yeow!" he yelled. He reached under the sink and turned the shutoff valve before screwing the hot-water lever back in place.

"Don't tell me," Nick said sarcastically. "This is the first time that's ever happened."

"Uh-huh," Roberto replied.

Unfortunately for Nick, his mishaps were far from over.

As they walked back down the hall, Nick unexplainably tripped. Stumbling, he instinctively reached for the hallway table to keep his balance.

But the table tipped under his weight, causing a ceramic statue to slide off. Nick lunged and caught the object just inches before it would have struck the floor.

He took one glance at the statue and shuddered. It was a ghoulish head that had bulging eyes, pointed eyebrows, funnel-shaped ears, no hair, and a grimace that revealed sharp fangs. *I almost wish it had broken, it's so ugly,* Nick thought. He straightened the table and carefully set down the statue.

As he turned to walk away, he heard a thud. The statue somehow had fallen to the floor. "Uh-oh." The left ear on the ceramic head had broken off.

"Look what you did!" Roberto yelled.

"I didn't do it!" Nick protested. "You saw me save the statue and put it back on the table. I don't know why it fell. I hope it wasn't valuable."

"I think it was old."

"Maybe we can glue it back." *No, I better wait until the Perezes get home and show them what happened. Probably whatever I make tonight will go toward the repair of this ugly thing.*

On the way back into the living room, Nick stopped by the front door and shook the handle a few times to make sure it was still locked. It was.

Minutes later, he was about to read more from *Day of the Dead* when the lamps flickered. The moment Nick put the book down, they stayed lit. He picked up the book only to have the lamps flicker again. "Okay, what's going on here?"

"I don't know," said Roberto. "That's the first time that's ever happened."

"Well, we certainly seem to be having a lot of firsts here tonight. Are you sure no one else is in this house?"

"You mean, like a person?"

"Of course I mean like a person."

"Nope," replied Roberto, "no one else."

"I want to see for myself."

They went from room to room, searching for what Nick suspected was some friend of Roberto's who was pulling jokes on the new sitter. But after making a clean sweep of the house—even checking under the beds and in the closets—Nick concluded the two definitely were alone—except for Spooky.

Nick turned on the TV and watched the Chicago Bulls play the Houston Rockets while Roberto drew pictures of tombstones. Early in the fourth quarter, Roberto fell asleep on the floor, so Nick carried him upstairs and put him to bed.

Walking back down, Nick noticed a bluish glow coming from the center hall. He tiptoed down the rest of the steps. At the bottom, he hesitated for a moment, then jumped into the hallway.

The glow vanished in an instant. *Must have been a police car going by outside,* he thought. *Come on, Nick, you're acting like a wimp. Every little thing spooks you . . . Hey, what just happened?* He flipped on the hall light. The statue of the chipped creepy-looking head was lying on its side on the hall table. *I know I didn't do that—unless it fell over when I jumped into the hallway.* He righted the statue. *I really hate this house.*

He returned to the living room to watch the exciting finish of the basketball game. The Bulls and Rockets were locked in a nail-biter as the lead seesawed back and forth. With five seconds left, Michael Jordan launched a shot from beyond the three-point arc that could win it for the Bulls. The ball soared toward the basket—

—and the TV went blank. "What? No! Not now!" Nick screamed. He leaped off his chair, fiddled with the TV buttons, and pounded on the set. The lamps in the room were lit, so he knew it wasn't a power failure.

Frustrated, he stepped away from the TV and felt something hard under his shoe. He bent down. *The plug to the TV set! How had it come out of the outlet?*

As Nick picked up the plug, he heard a hiss. Spooky bounded from the top of the TV onto Nick's back, digging his claws into Nick. "Ouch! Get off, you mangy cat!" Reaching around his back and twisting, Nick grabbed Spooky by the scruff of the cat's neck. He was ready to fling the cat away when Roberto walked into the room.

"Spooky!" Roberto hollered. "Get off him!"

The cat vaulted onto Roberto's shoulder and began purring. "I heard you yelling," Roberto told Nick, "so I came down to see what was going on."

"Your cat attacked me again—and I didn't step on

him," said Nick. "Why don't you take Spooky upstairs with you. Keep him away from me. I think he was playing with the cord to the TV . . . Oh, the game! I've got to see how it turned out." Nick plugged the cord into the outlet, returning the TV to life.

"What a game!" boomed the announcer. "Another one that went down to the wire. We'll see you Tuesday night when the Bulls take on the Cleveland Cavaliers. Good night from the United Center."

"The score! Give the score!" Nick stomped on the floor when a car commercial came on. "I missed the most exciting part of the game, and I don't even know who won."

Roberto shrugged and headed to bed, taking his cat with him.

After Nick slumped back to watch more TV, he had an unsettling feeling that he was being watched. He looked over both shoulders. Nothing. The feeling kept growing stronger. That's when he noticed the gargoyle statue on the shelf was glaring at him. So was the painting of the scowling woman . . . and the wood mask on the opposite wall . . . and the carved monster face on the mantel . . . and the two demon sculptures on the hutch. All were turned at exact angles, casting their cold stares directly at him.

Were they always pointed toward me or did Roberto turn them? He's a weird kid. This whole place is weird. Nick got up and turned the statues slightly so their gazes were no longer aimed at him.

Still, he couldn't shake the unsettling impression of being watched. He turned the TV volume down so he could hear any footsteps or breathing. *Someone is here. I can feel it.*

Suddenly, Nick felt a need to look out the window. *Uh-oh, what's that glow?*

It was the same blue light he had seen in the hallway earlier. As it began to pulsate, the glow took on the shape and size of a basketball. Slowly its features came into focus. *It's a head, a floating head!*

Too scared to run or look away, Nick kept his eyes glued on the grotesque face. The horrible head was the same as the ceramic statue that had broken in the hallway. Just like the statue in the hallway, the ghastly head in the window was also missing its left ear.

The glowing face sneered at Nick until the sitter finally broke free and ran into the kitchen. But then he saw the hideous face smirking at him from the kitchen window.

Screaming, Nick dashed into the dining room. As he ran past the window, he saw the maniacal face leering at him.

Nick tore free from its powerful gaze and sprinted into the bathroom. Seeing the shade was drawn on the window, he thought, *I'm safe in here.* But then a bluish glow spread across the wall. *No, not here too!* Nick looked at the mirror. The glowing face smiled back at him, displaying its jagged fangs.

"Aaaahhhh!" Nick lunged for the door, but it

wouldn't open. He pounded and kicked it. "Let me out! Let me out!" There was no way he could be trapped in here, because the door could only be locked from the inside. He fearfully glanced over his shoulder. The glowing face seemed to mock Nick's increasing terror and his futile efforts to flee.

Nick continued to pound and kick the door. Suddenly it swung open. He took one step—and confronted another face less than two feet away. "Aaaahhhh!"

"What is going on, Nick?" said Mr. Perez, who had opened the door. "Why are you banging on the door?"

"It was locked and I couldn't get out," Nick babbled. "There was a ghost in the mirror and in the windows. I have to tell you, Mr. Perez, this place is the creepiest house in town!"

"Settle down, boy, settle down. First, come out of the bathroom and let's go in the living room."

After the Perezes sat down with Nick, Mrs. Perez said, "My, Nick, you look like you've seen a ghost."

"I have," replied Nick. "I saw his ugly face. He looks just like the statue in the hallway. I don't care if you think I'm crazy, but his head was glowing and it was floating."

Mrs. Perez looked at her husband knowingly and nodded. At her urging, Nick told them of all the peculiar mishaps and frightening incidents he had experienced. "You probably think I belong in a mental hospital, but everything I said is the truth."

"We know you're telling the truth," she said.

"You do?"

"Yes, and we owe you an apology. You see, Nick, our house has a ghost. He's been here ever since we moved in. We don't know who he is or why he's here.

"About a month after we moved in, I was sitting up late one night when all of a sudden the front door—which was locked—flew open, then immediately shut itself again. Naturally, I was surprised. Then the door to the utility room began to rattle as if the wind was blowing—yet there were no open windows.

"We Perezes have a strong belief in the supernatural. Although I was a little concerned, I wondered if this was caused by a ghost. So I said out loud, 'While you're at it, could you open a couple of windows?' Two windows in the living room sprang up by themselves.

"About a week later, every cupboard in the kitchen opened by itself. I said, 'Now close them.' One by one, they shut by themselves.

"Every now and then the ghost lets us know he's around. He'll move a statue or make a noise. But he's never been mean or scared us. We're not afraid of him. He *can* be a pest, but we consider him part of the family."

"He's merely an unfortunate soul caught between his past and the present," Mr. Perez added. "We've learned to share our house with him. He's never made his presence known to any other sitter—or anybody else for that matter. It's obvious to me that he's been playing games with you. The ghost was behind all the incidents you experienced tonight—even the ones with the cat."

"Although you're probably a very fine boy and a good baby-sitter, our ghost obviously doesn't like you," Mrs. Perez said. "We're so sorry he pestered you."

She reached out and placed Nick's hand in hers. With a sigh she said, "It's probably best if you don't baby-sit here anymore."

Nick stood up and retorted, "No offense, Mrs. Perez. But you couldn't pay me enough money to baby-sit in this house ever again!"

THE SKELETON GHOST

Taylor Mason woke up with a start. An uneasy feeling crept slowly through her bones.

The fifteen-year-old baby-sitter sat up on the couch as her eyes darted around the darkened family room. *Everything seems okay,* she thought. *It's quiet.* In fact, it was so quiet she could hear her heart pounding much louder and faster than normal.

Taylor glanced at her watch. It glowed 12:35 A.M. The Weinsteins wouldn't be home for another half hour. *Why do I feel so edgy?* she wondered. *Maybe it's the geometry midterm. I've been studying for hours but I just know I'm going to flunk it.*

The tired sitter yawned and fluffed up the cushions on the couch where she had been dozing for the past hour. The Weinsteins wouldn't mind her sleeping on the couch. It was so big and comfy that they joked that their kids—Becca, nine, Bree, eight, and Brian, six—spent more time sleeping there than in their own rooms.

But on this night, the kids were in bed. As Taylor laid her head on a cushy pillow, she spotted a female figure in a long nightgown standing in the doorway. Although the figure looked slightly taller than a child, Taylor assumed it was Becca. "What do you want, honey?" she asked the girl.

She didn't receive an answer. The figure glided effortlessly toward her. Taylor rubbed her eyes and fumbled for the switch to the lamp next to the couch, but she couldn't quite reach it and was too lazy to get up.

"Becca, are you sleepwalking again?" Without responding, the figure snuggled up to the sitter on the couch. "So you want to sleep with me, huh?" said Taylor. "Okay."

Taylor threw her arm around the figure's waist and immediately jerked it away. The body felt cold and bony, not warm and cuddly. Taylor sat up and turned on the lamp—and stared into the gruesome face of death.

There, lying on its back on the couch, only inches from Taylor, was a skeleton whose bones were covered by a gray, wafer-thin layer of wrinkled skin! The face had only dark holes where eyes, ears, and a nose used to be. The mouth was frozen in a ghastly grin. White limp hair flopped down from the top of its skull to the collar of a plain beige nightgown. The skeleton began to rise.

Taylor soared off the couch, shrieking in stark terror. Her flailing arms knocked over the lamp, throwing the room once again into darkness.

Still screaming, Taylor backed away, bumping into furniture as she stumbled out of the family room. The panicky sitter backpedaled until she collided with another smaller figure behind her in the darkness. Taylor wheeled around and screeched even louder.

The smaller figure yelled too.

"Becca, is that you?" Taylor gasped.

"Uh-huh," replied a timid voice.

Taylor groped for the switch on the wall and turned on the hall light. They both ran into each other's arms.

"I heard screaming and it woke me up," said Becca.

"That was me," Taylor admitted.

Bree tottered sleepily down the hall, rubbing her eyes. "Who was yelling?"

"Everything is fine," Taylor fibbed. "I want you both to go back to your room. Check on your brother to make sure he's still asleep. I'll look in on you both in just a minute."

While the girls did what they were told, Taylor ran into the kitchen and grabbed a broom out of the pantry. She tiptoed to the family room and, with the broom raised high, flipped on the ceiling light. The lamp lay on the floor, cracked in several places. A chair leaned on its back and a potted plant rested on its side. Taylor's tensed-up body relaxed when she saw no sign of the hideous-looking skeleton. Bravely, she searched behind the curtains and under the furniture in the other rooms, including the recently remodeled wing of the sprawling nineteenth-century house. At every possible hiding place, she wondered if the ghost was lying in wait, ready to spring on its victim.

Satisfied that the skeleton ghost was gone, Taylor checked on Brian, saw he was asleep, then went into the girls' room.

"Taylor, you're scaring me," said Bree. "What happened? Why were you screaming?"

"I thought I saw a . . ." *Be careful what you say,* Taylor told herself. *You'll frighten Becca and Bree.* "I thought I saw a shadow. But now I realize I was dreaming, that's all. I fell asleep on the couch and had a nightmare. I'm really sorry I scared you two."

Returning to the family room, Taylor flipped on all the lights and straightened up the mess. *How am I going to explain the broken lamp? I guess I'll tell the Weinsteins the truth. But what is the truth? Did I have a nightmare? It seemed too real to be a bad dream. But if it was real, what was it? Will it return?*

The trembling sitter perched on the edge of the couch and turned on the television. She felt safer surrounded by noise and lights. Although she tried to pay attention to a *Brady Bunch* rerun, her mind kept replaying those appalling moments when she had touched that disgusting ghost.

Movement suddenly caught her eye. Taylor jumped up and looked toward the hallway. Becca was leaning against the door. "Becca, you startled me. How long have you been standing there?"

"About a half minute. You saw it, didn't you?"

"Saw what?"

Before Becca could respond, Taylor heard a key turning in the kitchen door. "Your parents are home," Taylor whispered. "You're going to get me in trouble if they see you're still up. Go back to bed and pretend to be asleep."

Minutes later, Taylor was apologizing to the Weinsteins for accidentally knocking over the lamp. "I had a nightmare when I was asleep on the couch," she told them. "I'll pay for a replacement."

"That's okay," said Mrs. Weinstein. "Now I can go buy a lamp I really like. Forget about it."

During the brief ride home, Taylor wondered what Becca had meant when she said, "You saw it, didn't you?" *Had she seen the skeleton ghost too? Or was she referring to something else—maybe other spirits in the house?* Taylor couldn't wait to talk to Becca.

Two weeks later, Taylor sat for the Weinstein kids again. The moment their parents left the house, Taylor cornered Becca alone in the kitchen and asked, "What did you mean the other night when you asked me if I saw it? What's 'it'?"

Becca wavered, not sure she wanted to say anything. Finally, she blurted, "Did you see a ghost— a skeleton ghost of a woman?"

"Yes, I did. How did you know?"

"I've seen her too. She's gray, all skin and bones."

"You've seen her? Where? When?"

"She visited me about two months ago. She came right out of the wall—the one between our room and the remodeled part of the house—and stood at the foot of my bed."

Taylor blinked at the stunning news and sat down at the kitchen table. "Becca, weren't you terrified?"

"At first I was so scared I couldn't even scream. But then the ghost bowed her head and held her hands. I think it was her way of saying she wasn't here to hurt anyone. Then she came closer. I was still afraid, so I screamed and woke up Bree. Mom and Dad ran into my room. When I told them what happened, they said it was only a nightmare. I believed them. But then she came back two more times. I think she knew I was still scared, so she never came closer than my bed."

"Have the other kids seen her?"

Becca shook her head. "Bree thinks I'm making it up. So do Mom and Dad. I stopped saying anything to them because I heard them saying that they might take me to a head doctor." Becca reached out and squeezed the sitter's hand. "Taylor, I'm not imagining this. You *did* see her, didn't you?"

Taylor nodded. "I wish I hadn't, but I know I did. I touched her. She was cold, icy cold—the kind of cold that sends shivers through your body. How can you live in this house with that ghost here? How can you even sleep at night?"

"She's awful to look at, but she doesn't mean to scare anyone. I kind of feel sorry for her."

"I hope I never see her again."

After thinking for a moment, Becca suggested, "Let's try to talk to her."

"What do you mean?"

Becca stood up, her voice brimming with excitement. "Taylor, let's have a séance! Maybe we can get her to appear so we can find out what she wants."

"You don't know anything about conducting a séance."

"Sure I do. I saw it on TV. I'll get Bree and Brian. They'll think it'll be cool to make a ghost appear."

"The kids could get scared silly, and I could get into big trouble with your folks."

"Bree and Brian won't be afraid."

"I don't know about this, Becca."

"Come on, Taylor, it'll be fun. Besides, how else are you going to find out who she is?"

Against her better judgment, Taylor soon found herself in the darkened family room. She and the Weinstein kids sat in a circle on the floor. A lit candle glowed in the center.

"Well, Miss Ghost, if you'd like to talk to us, we're here to listen," said Becca. When Brian began to giggle, Becca snapped, "Quiet, Brian." Then in a more pleasant voice, Becca said, "Miss Ghost, don't mind him. We're serious. Let's hear from you."

About thirty seconds later, the four of them were

jolted by a series of loud bangs in the room. Brian leaped to his feet. "I'm scared."

Taylor quickly got up and turned on the light. Giving Brian a comforting hug, she said, "It's all right, honey. Those bangs are just thunder," she lied.

"But I don't see any lightning," said Bree, gazing out the window.

"Then they're sonic booms—noises made by jets when they fly faster than the speed of sound," said Taylor, trying to mask her fear over the alarming noise. "The séance is over. Bree, take Brian to his room and watch TV. I want to talk to Becca alone."

After the two kids had left, Taylor turned to Becca, who was still sitting on the floor, her legs crossed over each other. Her eyes were closed and her hands lay in her lap, palms up. In an eerily deep voice, Becca uttered, "I don't like it here."

Putting her hands on her hips, Taylor growled, "Okay, Becca, that's enough. The séance is over."

"My name is Mary. Mary Hayden."

Becca was talking out of the side of her mouth. She sounded like a gravelly-voiced elderly woman with an English accent.

"Becca, that's an impressive voice, but let's put a stop to this. We've scared the kids, so knock it off."

"I do not know this Becca of whom you speak. I am Mary Hayden from Portland by way of Surrey."

Intrigued by the way Becca could make her voice sound so different and adult, Taylor sat down next to her and played along. "So, Mary, what do you do?"

"I am in charge of this house. It is too much responsibility. I must do it all alone."

"How old are you?"

"I was born in 1798."

"Where?"

"Surrey, England. That is where I wish I could be."

"Why?"

"Because I am unhappy here in Portland. I haven't seen my husband, Tom, in so long."

"Where is he?"

"Tom went away on his whaling ship, the *Saint Beatrice*. He said he would be back, but it's been a long, long time. I have all of this responsibility. I must tend the garden and the flock. It's April, time for shearing the sheep."

"Oh, you have a farm?"

"Yes, and I must do everything myself. I'm so tired. I wish someone would take care of me, hold me and comfort me."

Taylor was enthralled by Becca's remarkable imitation and imagination. *Let's see where this goes,* the sitter thought.

"Are you aware you're dead?" Taylor asked.

"Don't talk like that to me."

"What year is it?"

"1847."

"Actually, it's 1997, but why quibble over 150 years? So, Mary, why are you talking to me?"

"I want you to help me with the farm. It's too much. I can't get help from the town."

"Don't you have relatives? Children? Friends?"

"My children have gone away. I'm all alone."

From the other room, Brian let out a wail and then ran into the hallway. "Taylor! Bree just hit me!"

"Becca, you are really good, but it's time to end this act," said Taylor. "I have to break up a fight." The sitter got up and headed for the hallway.

For a fleeting moment, she thought she saw the skeleton ghost hovering behind Becca. But when Taylor blinked, she saw nothing. *My mind is playing tricks on me.*

After acting as peacemaker for Brian and Bree, Taylor returned to the family room. Becca was on the floor, looking perplexed. "Where is everyone, Taylor? Why are the lights on? What happened?"

"You put on quite a performance, pretending to be the ghost. You almost had me believing it."

"Taylor, I don't remember anything after hearing those bangs. It's like I fell asleep, only I wasn't really. I think I was in a trance."

"Becca, you can stop now. You're very good. Your voice sounded like an old English woman. It's hard to believe it came from such a young girl. You're a born actress."

Becca rose to her feet and squeezed Taylor's arm. "I wasn't acting! Tell me what I said!"

"Enough is enough," Taylor barked. "You know darn well what you said. You made it all up."

Becca's eyes flared in anger. "Yeah, sure, just like I made the walls bang. How do you explain that,

Miss Know-It-All?" Becca stomped off to her room.

Taylor fell onto the couch, picked up the remote, and channel surfed. Meanwhile, she carried on a conversation in her mind. *Could the ghost have talked through Becca? No, that's ridiculous. But what about the banging? Maybe they really were sonic booms. Did I see the ghost again tonight? Quit thinking about it, Taylor. For all you know you never saw a real ghost in the first place. Maybe it was just a dream. Maybe Becca is a mind reader or something. Oh, geez, that's just as crazy as admitting a ghost talked through Becca. Mary Hayden, huh. I wonder if there really is such a person.*

The following Saturday, Taylor was slurping from a bowl of Cheerios at the breakfast table across from her father. She noticed a story on the front page of the paper that he was reading:

REMAINS OF OLD WHALING SHIP DISCOVERED

Divers Tuesday confirmed that they have found the hull and other artifacts of a Portland whaling ship that was lost at sea in 1847.

While making a scientific survey of the ocean bottom two hundred miles (322 km) northeast of Maine, divers came across the submerged hull of a wreck last week. Upon further examination, experts determined the ship was a whaler that had set sail from

Portland 150 years ago.

The ship, the *Saint Beatrice*, was captained by Tom Hayden . . .

"Oh, my gosh! Un-be-liev-able!" Taylor yelled.

"Yikes," said her dad, shoving himself away from the table. "You made me spill my coffee."

"Sorry, Daddy, but I'm freaked right now. I'll tell you all about it later." She grabbed the front page and bolted out the door.

Taylor sprinted the four blocks to the Weinsteins' house and rang the bell. Mrs. Weinstein answered the door. "Taylor, what are you doing here?"

"Please don't take this the wrong way, but I think your house is haunted!"

"Not you too." Mrs. Weinstein groaned.

"What do you mean?"

Mrs. Weinstein opened the door and motioned for Taylor to come inside. Sitting at the kitchen table were Becca, Bree, Brian, and Mr. Weinstein.

"Hi, everyone," Taylor said. "Becca, it looks like you've been crying."

"I have. I saw the skeleton ghost again last night—except nobody believes me."

"What happened?"

"I was in the family room when I saw the plant on the floor by the TV start to move across the floor. I yelled for Mom and Dad to come quick, but when they did, the plant had already tipped over. They said I did it."

Mrs. Weinstein interrupted, "Potted plants simply don't move by themselves."

Becca continued. "We got into a shouting match and I was sent to my room for a time-out. That's when the banging started. You know, the same noise we heard when you baby-sat us last time. It was real loud. The walls shook. It was coming from my room, so naturally Mom and Dad thought I was doing it. They yelled at me to stop it, and I told them I wasn't doing it. Then it stopped."

"I don't see where this is any of Taylor's concern, Becca," grumbled Mr. Weinstein.

"I might be able to shed some light on things if you let Becca finish her story," Taylor said.

After getting a halfhearted nod from her father, Becca continued. "Later that night, I woke up and felt someone get in bed with me. I thought it was Bree. She was hogging the pillow, so I rolled over and kicked her. Only it wasn't Bree. It was the skeleton ghost. She was ice-cold and icky. I panicked and screamed and woke up the whole house. The ghost shook her head and disappeared. Now Mom and Dad say I have to go to a head doctor and that I've upset Bree and Brian with my stories."

Mr. Weinstein turned to Taylor and pointedly asked, "Since you're here, can you explain why you allowed Becca to hold that silly séance last week? You should've known better, especially with children that young."

"I understand why you and Mrs. Weinstein might

be upset by the séance." Taylor put her hands on the table and leaned toward Mr. Weinstein. "But you need to know one thing. I saw the skeleton ghost too."

The Weinsteins folded their arms, clearly annoyed and unbelieving.

"That's why I agreed to the séance," Taylor explained. "At first I thought Becca was putting on an act. But now I believe the ghost talked to me— through Becca."

"This is absurd!" Mr. Weinstein thundered, throwing his hands in the air.

Becca had been hanging on every word Taylor said. Now she asked, "The ghost talked to you through me?"

"Yes," Taylor answered. "I'm sorry I doubted you, Becca. But the séance worked. I'm positive the ghost of Mary Hayden was speaking to me."

Mrs. Weinstein slapped the table. "Now I'm getting really concerned. Taylor, maybe you should leave."

"Please hear me out," Taylor pleaded. Quickly, she told them about her frightening encounter with the ghost—a ghost that matched the description Becca later gave her. She told them about the loud bangs and what Mary Hayden's ghost had said to her during the séance.

"Why don't you think Becca made it up?" asked Mr. Weinstein.

Taylor held out the newspaper and placed it triumphantly on the table. "Look at this! Mary's ghost told me that she was waiting for her husband, Tom, to return from the sea. She said he was captain of a ship called the *Saint Beatrice* which left Portland in 1847 and never returned. How would Becca have known anything about the sunken ship or the captain's name? The shipwreck wasn't discovered until after the séance."

Mrs. Weinstein nervously tapped the table with her long fingernails. "This sounds like pure fiction."

"Yes, it does, except it happens to be true," said Taylor. "Mr. and Mrs. Weinstein, this house of yours is haunted. The ghost is very scary to look at, but she's not mean. She's lonely. I think she's seeking comfort."

"If there is a ghost—and that's a mighty big if— why didn't she make herself known to us before?" asked Mrs. Weinstein. "We've lived here for six years."

"I don't know. Maybe the remodeling of your house stirred her up."

"That's right, Dad," said Becca. "The skeleton ghost first appeared right after the workers started remodeling the house."

"I'm not ready to believe this," said Mr. Weinstein. "Other than the fact that Bree and Brian heard the banging too, you have no other witnesses to this so-called ghost."

Bree began to tremble and anxiously rubbed her hands. "If I tell you something, Daddy, do you promise you won't send me to the head doctor?"

"What is it, sugar?"

"I saw the ghost last night. I didn't say anything because I was afraid you'd get mad at me like you did Becca and you'd make me go to the doctor too."

"What did you see?"

"A ghost that looked like skin and bones with hair. She was floating above my bed after Becca screamed. The ghost was there and then she was gone." Turning to her sister, Bree added, "I'm sorry I didn't say anything about it, Becca. But I didn't want to get into trouble like you did."

Mrs. Weinstein reached over and kissed Bree and Becca. "I'm so sorry, kids. Dad and I have never believed in ghosts. We were worried that you were seeing things that weren't there. That's a very scary thing for parents."

"Imagine how scary it is for us," said Becca.

Feeling relieved that the Weinsteins were beginning to believe the girls, the sitter asked, "Do you know anything about the history of the house?"

"Not really," said Mr. Weinstein. "All the historical society knew was that it was built sometime in the early 1840s and that it had farmland behind it."

"That's consistent with what Mary told me," said Taylor.

"I don't want to live with a ghost, Mommy," Brian whined. "Make her go away."

"I'd love nothing better," said Mrs. Weinstein. "But how?"

"Why not hold another séance?" Taylor suggested. "We'll talk to Mary—through Becca—and ask her to leave for good."

The Weinsteins reluctantly agreed. Later that night, Taylor and the family sat in a candlelit circle. Becca then said softly, "Mary Hayden, please speak to us. We're your friends."

The hutch began to rattle, shaking the glasses. Then several loud booms rocked the room, causing Mrs. Weinstein and Brian to squeal with fright.

"It's okay, everyone," Taylor said soothingly. "Let's keep holding hands."

Shortly after Becca closed her eyes, her back became ramrod straight. Suddenly she began speaking out of the side of her mouth in the voice of an elderly woman with an English accent.

"I have nobody to write to, nobody to visit. I don't like it here. I want my husband," the voice complained.

"Mary, is that you?" asked Taylor.

"Yes."

"Captain Tom died," Taylor said. "His ship sank a long time ago, in 1847. You have died too. You're a ghost now, Mary. You don't have to stay here anymore. Don't you want to be with your husband?"

Ignoring what Taylor had said, Mary, through Becca's voice, complained, "I can't do it all myself. I need to get some women from town to help with the spinning."

"But there is a new family living in this house, and

143

they're taking care of everything," Taylor explained. "You don't have to worry anymore. You can go now."

"Back to England?"

"Anywhere you wish."

"What about the animals?"

Even though there were no animals at the Weinstein residence, Taylor fibbed, "They'll be looked after. You can go now and be with your husband. Call for him."

"Tom? Tom? Is that you? Oh, Tom, I've missed you so."

After a minute of silence, Taylor asked, "Mary, are you and Tom together now?"

"Yes, he's taking me back to Surrey. Isn't that nice?"

Becca slouched her back and opened her eyes. "What happened?" she asked in her own voice.

"I think we've heard the last of the ghost of Mary Hayden," Taylor replied. "She's finally found the love and comfort she's been seeking all these years."